THE COUNTRY RHYMES OF
HUGH PORTER

THE BARD OF MONEYSLANE
Born c. 1780

THE FOLK POETS OF ULSTER

TITLES IN THE SERIES

VOLUME ONE
THE COUNTRY RHYMES OF
HUGH PORTER
THE BARD OF MONEYSLANE

VOLUME TWO
THE COUNTRY RHYMES OF
JAMES ORR
THE BARD OF BALLYCARRY

VOLUME THREE
THE COUNTRY RHYMES OF
SAMUEL THOMSON
THE BARD OF CARNGRANNY

PRETANI PRESS

VOLUME ONE
THE FOLK POETS OF ULSTER

THE COUNTRY RHYMES OF

HUGH PORTER

THE BARD OF MONEYSLANE
Born c. 1780

WITH AN INTRODUCTION BY
AMBER ADAMS & J.R.R. ADAMS

First published by Pretani Press, 1992
78 Abbey Street, Bangor BT20 4JB

This book has received financial assistance under
the Cultural Traditions Programme which aims to
encourage acceptance and understanding of
cultural diversity.

Design and typesetting by Pegasus Design Consultants, Belfast.
Photography by Gemini, Belfast.
Antiques supplied by Robert Huffam, Carrickfergus.
Original maps by Alison Hogg
Printed in Northern Ireland by
W. & G. Baird Ltd.

ISBN 0 948868 17 1

PRETANI PRESS

CONTENTS

vii	The folk poets of Ulster
ix	Introduction
xvii	Identifications of dedications
xix	Subscribers' names
xxviii	The author's dedication to the Right Hon the Earl of Moira
xxix	The author's preface
1	To the Reverend T. T.
4	To the Reverend T. T.
7	To Reverend T. T. after an absence of some weeks
10	On the eclipse of the sun, 11 February, 1804
13	To the Reverend T. T.
15	To disappointment
17	To Reverend B. W. M.
19	A song on marriage
22	The bard
27	On seeing his name in Robinson's book of poems, with "Esq." added to it
30	The muse dismissed
31	The muse returns
35	To the Prince Regent
37	The making of a man
40	On the appointment of the Earl of Moira, to be Governor General and Commander of the forces in India
42	An advertisement
44	The drunkard's fate
47	Crime and punishment
52	Sonnet to friendship
53	An epistle to Bonaparte
56	To the Reverend T. T. from his pony
60	To W. B. Esq. The humble petition of Hugh Porter
62	To J. J. a brither rhymer
64	On being asked why poets are poor and seldom contented
66	On the supposed loss of a friend
67	A soliloquy written in a storm
69	Sonnet to death
70	An address to poverty

73	To the Reverend T. T.
74	To one who demanded interest for lending five shillings a few days
76	To Miss —— ——
79	Written the next morning after having dined and supped with the Rev Messrs T. and B.
81	To the Most Noble the Marquis of Downshire
82	On the accidental death of a favourite pointer
83	The epitaph
84	To T. J. T. Esq.
87	The last speech, and dying lamentation of Ballyward Lake
90	On being alone in the Rev T. T.'s parlour
91	To the Rev D**** M*****
93	To the Rev T***** M**** R***
96	Answer to Burns' "Lovely Jean"
98	Reflections occasioned by the illness of the Rev T***** T****
100	On his recovery
101	To the President and other members of the Rathfriland Book Society
104	Answer from the Society to Tisander
105	To Mr G. A. who proposed him as an Honorary Member
108	To the memory of the late Thomas, Lord Bishop of Dromore
110	The profligate
111	To His Grace the Duke of ——
112	Epigram to a liar
112	An epitaph on a miser
112	Another
113	On a spendthrift
113	On a sluggard
113	To a friend in trouble
115	Erin's welcome to the Earl of Moira
116	To the Reverend T. T. on the beginning of the year 1812
118	To Walter Scott, Esq.
120	To the Reverend T. T. on the death of his eldest son
122	A concluding address to the reader

POEMS BY PATRICK BRONTË

124	Extract from 'The Irish cabin'
126	Extract from 'Epistle to the Rev J—— B——'
128	Glossary

THE FOLK POETS OF ULSTER

The vernacular poetical tradition in Ulster was part of a much broader literary movement focussed in Scotland and culminating in the work of Robert Burns at the end of the eighteenth century. This virile Ulster tradition, much of it written in lowland Scots, has its beginnings early in the eighteenth century, before the work of Burns.

The works produced by the writers in this tradition were rescued by the late John Hewitt, in his book *Rhyming Weavers* (first published in 1974). This caused the value of these poets to be recognised by local historians, giving as they do a peasant's eye view of local life and customs, attitudes to religion and politics and such matters.

The purpose of this series is not to interpret or explain the poems, but to make them accessible once more, and to provide for each poet a biographical sketch. Some, nearly all, of the original volumes are extremely rare, and only found in the larger scholarly libraries.

Where the poets were prolific and produced several volumes, a selection has been made which prefers those written in Ulster-Scots rather than standard English, and which cover themes of local and historical interest.

The main era of publication was from c.1790 to c.1840, in the immediate wake of Burns' first edition of 1786, and during this period dozens of Ulster poets (notably from the counties of Down and Antrim) produced volumes of verse, mainly supported by subscriptions (pre-publication orders), overwhelmingly from friends and neighbours.

The vigorous Ulster-Scots of these poets will be difficult reading for even fluent speakers of modern vernacular. It is recommended that in reading those poems the full depth of meaning will not be transmitted unless a dialect dictionary (e.g. *The Concise Scots Dictionary*) is used frequently - even for those words which look familiar.

Series Editors:
J. R. R. Adams
P. S. Robinson

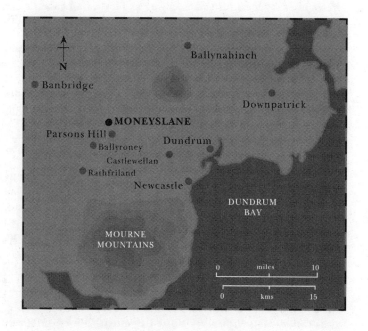

INTRODUCTION

And thirdly, in the style appears
The accent o' my early years,
Which is nor Scotch nor English either,
But part o' baith mix'd up thegither:
Yet its the sort my neighbours use,
Wha think shoon prettier far than shoes.

Very little is known about the life of Hugh Porter, the author of these poems. A poor linen weaver from Moneyslane in the parish of Drumballyroney and Drumgooland, he was born about 1780. His early education was poor - as was common at the time, he would have attended a local hedge school, and acquired only basic literacy. He began to read, and gradually began to write, particularly verses. These were originally never meant for publication, but to please himself and a few friends.

Then in 1799 he took the step that was to lead to general recognition. He presented a poem to the Rev Thomas Tighe, the local rector. This was a shrewd move, for Tighe had very good literary connections indeed and in his home at Parson's Hill frequently entertained these learned friends. At the head of this local literary circle was Thomas Percy, Bishop of Dromore, the author of *Reliques of ancient English poetry* and a man acquainted with the most eminent literary people of the day. He had been a member of the Johnsonian circle, and continued throughout his long life to maintain a voluminous correspondence with the literary giants of the British Isles. On coming to Dromore he set about encouraging local talent. Though his literary circle extended far beyond his diocese, there were several local literary men of eminence.

These included Henry Boyd, the vicar of Rathfriland, who was well known for his translations of Dante, and Thomas Stott ('Hafiz') of Dromore, who wrote countless poems for the Belfast and English newspapers but whose chief claim

[ix]

to fame today is that he was ridiculed by Lord Byron as 'grovelling Stott'. There were also more minor talents, such as Hugh Porter himself. So when Porter presented his poem to Tighe, (followed by others), he became known to Bishop Percy.

This placed him in a chain of intellectual endeavour, admittedly as one of the lower links. Above Porter was his patron, Thomas Tighe. He in turn was familiar with such as Henry Boyd. Above that again was the eminent Bishop, and via him there was access to the London literary scene. It must have been an exciting time for Porter.

In the early years of the nineteenth century Porter published some of his poems in the local newspapers, under the pen-name of 'A County Down Weaver'. (He later used the pen-name 'Tisander', probably given to him by Boyd). 'An epistle to Bonaparte' appeared in January 1808, and 'The drunkard' in February of the same year. He was extremely excited by this, writing an elated and self-mocking poem addressed to 'J. J. a Brither rhymer' (possibly James Jackson of Imdel).

> *O printin'! printin'! cream o' craft!*
> *Ye'll sen' me - whar? alaft, alaft;*
> *Ye'll mak' me - what? I marvel aft,*
>   *A - a - a - poet;*
> *O! O! I fear 'twill drive me daft,*
>   *Just thinkin' o' it.*

> *An author! aye, aye, there's the matter*
> *That's better boy, better an' better; -*
> *What am I - no a human creature -*
>   *For see! I'm climbin',*
> *Up - up - I'm up, it's past a clatter,*
>   *And I'm past rhymin'.*

These few years, from about 1807 - 1810, were his years of 'hopes and fears', when he felt that he might make it as a poet. He also obviously felt aggrieved by the fact that he did not, writing poems about the hard life of poets.

> *One reason that poets are poor,*
> *Misfortunes do often await them;*
> *Another, as solid I'm sure,*
> *They're simple, and most people cheat them.*

He had obviously also fallen out with his beloved patron Tighe for some reason.

> *But now, my friends, the feeling few*
> *Yield my enfeebl'd frame to you;*
> *Now, desperation darts me thro',*
> *And worse than all,*
> *The generous T**** has left me too,*
> *To stand or fall.*

Then members of Bishop Percy's circle encouraged Tighe to edit and publish a collection of Porter's poems in book form. This caused the good rector some considerable embarrassment, for, as the reader of the book will soon become aware, a large number of the poems were hymns of praise to him (when they were not complaints of neglect). He delayed for more than two years, (in November 1811 the book was announced as ready for the press, and subscriptions were being solicited, yet it did not appear until 1813), and Porter's high hopes turned to despair.

Not only was Porter suffering from dashed literary hopes, but his health was failing, and he was unable to support himself and family by weaving. He needed money, and finally Tighe organised the publication of the book 'to help to exhilarate the evening of the author's life by raising a little fund for that purpose, in a manner the most agreeable to his feelings, by exhibiting the energies and grateful effusions of his own mind'.

As was common at that time, subscribers in advance for the volume were sought, and Tighe used all his influence. The result was a list of over 600 people, some of the highest station in life, as well as many local people. There were more than forty titled subscribers, and some fifteen

Cambridge dons - Tighe had obviously used his old university contacts. It is noticeable, however, that other weaver poets were absent - Porter, while a humble member of the Percy/Tighe circle, had only a limited acquaintance with his peers in other parts of Ulster. Perhaps as a poet with a patron he was not felt to be independent enough by the rest of his breed. Unlike many of them, as well, he was no radical.

However, at least he had the pleasure of launching his book in some style. Not all, indeed very few, local poets came near this. The unfortunate Mr William Percy (no relation to the Bishop), whose *Essays in verse* were published in the same year, had to resort to different means, as the following advertisement shows.

> *Mr Percy, by advice of a number of friends, hereby announces his determination this day to substitute the hours from 7 till 9 in the evening in the room of from 10 till 12 in the morning, to READ and RECITE extracts from his intended publication of* Essays *chiefly in verse, the other arrangements from 1 till 3, and from 4 till 6, remain unaltered. Subscriptions without money will be taken from such as may wish, after a candid hearing, to encourage the work. N.B. Admission from 7 till 9 evening - Gentlemen 1s 8d, ladies 10d.*

This was followed by another advertisement.

> *Mr Percy most pathetically solicits the patronage of all his well-wishers, both in town and country. Why do they not call at the News-letter Office for a supply thereof, agreeably to his request in his proposals. He most humbly proposes to solicit the individual patronage, personally, of every town in Ulster.*

To Porter's volume Tighe added a glossary, rather unusual in a volume of weaver poetry. It was probably felt necessary, in view of the eminent status of many of the subscribers. It seems to have been compiled using the glossary contained in the standard contemporary editions of Burns' poems, adding such words as were not included in that list.

Porter had all the awe of a self-educated man at books. When he first entered Parson's Hill he was amazed at Tighe's books:

> I entered in your parlour door,
> And as I stalked owre the floor,
> I saw - but sic a sight before
>   I ne'er had seen,
> A thousand beuks I'm sure, and more,
>   Surpriz'd my een.

He was grateful for the loan of books from Tighe's library, and it was a friend of Tighe, Gilbert Adams, who allowed him the use of the volumes in the Rathfriland Book Society, when he did not have the price of admission. He also seems to have kept up to a certain extent with current events, mentioning personages as diverse as Napoleon Bonaparte and Spencer Perceval, the assassinated British Prime Minister. The contemporary poets mentioned by him - William Hamilton Drummond, Henry Boyd, Thomas Stott ('Hafiz'), Thomas Romney Robinson and so on would have been familiar to him from his conversations at Parson's Hill.

He was proud indeed to see his own name in the list of subscribers to Robinson's *Juvenile poems* when these were published in 1806. No doubt Tighe had paid for him, adding Esq. after his name.

> My up-start brethren, ane an' a',
> Frae Dingle down to Derry wa',
> Say, if you ever heard or saw
>   A thing sae queer,
> As next to naebody ava
>   Become a Squire.

Despite his friendship with Tighe, (at least at times), and the access this gave him to a wider literary circle, he was always conscious of his lowly station and poor circumstances. It would probably be true to say that his acquaintance with better things actually left him more unhappy than he would otherwise have been.

> O ye! wha bask in Fortune's ray,
> An' row in rowth, frae day to day,
>   Wha's path-way, pleasure paves;
> How (shame upon ye), can ye stan'
> An' heap preferment on a clan
>   O saucy, senseless knaves?
> An' frien'less leave the simple Bard
>   Amang the rustic boors,
> An' say his palate's no prepar'd
>   For dainty bits like yours;
> For nature, the creature
>   Has form'd plebeian, rude -
> Not so, we - for lo! we
>   Are noble, great an' good.

So here we have Hugh Porter of Moneyslane: poor, hearing all the literary gossip while dining with Tighe and Boyd on good food and fine wine one day, eating potatoes in his cabin the next, contemplating a future that seemed hopeless, a fame that he would never have. It must have seemed doubly unjust, for Tighe had had another protégé, also at one time a neighbour in the same parish. This person had been encouraged by Tighe to go to Cambridge.

THE BRONTË CONNECTION

This other person was Patrick Brontë, the father of the Brontë sisters. Brontë was born at Imdel, a townland neighbouring Moneyslane, in 1777. At an early age he was apprenticed to a blacksmith, and afterwards to a weaver at Banbridge. He was befriended by the Rev Andrew Harshaw, a Presbyterian, who allowed him access to his library. In 1793 he became schoolmaster at Glascar, and in

1798 schoolmaster at Drumballyroney parish school, of which parish the Rev Thomas Tighe was of course vicar.

In addition to the day-school, he had a class for private tuition, which met in Tighe's drawing-room. Tighe encouraged him to go to St John's College, Cambridge (his old alma mater), which he entered in 1802. To the other poor weaver and literary enthusiast from the area, who was also a frequent visitor at Parson's Hill, this must have been a bitter blow. It was probably this which led to the nervous disorders and despair which overcame him shortly afterwards.

Indeed it may have been the publication of Patrick Brontë's *Cottage poems* in England in 1811 which gave some impetus to the movement to get Porter's poems published (two extracts from this work are included in the present volume). Tighe and his friends would not have been unaware of the printing of their protégé's first book. Indeed the volume contains a poem entitled 'The Irish Cabin', which describes a humble cottage in the Mournes.

The two poets who became acquainted with Tighe at about the same time could not have had more different subsequent histories. Brontë went on to father the famous sisters and become part of the heritage industry in two countries. Porter lapsed into obscurity, but an obscurity not as deep as that suffered by 'J. J. a brither rhymer' from Imdel. A few years later, in 1819, Porter was referred to, though not by name, by John M'Kinley.

> *All hail, ye patrons of the hapless bard,*
> *From whom e'en weakest merit meets reward!*
> *Where lonely Hilltown looks o'er silver Ban,*
> *That laves Rathfriland, winds through Moneyslan,*
> *See classic Boyd, and philanthropic Tighe,*
> *Disclaim the pride of scornful scrutiny -*
> *Protect and partonize the rustic lay,*
> *And usher drooping genius into day!*

Porter wrote in a number of metres, but the most characteristic is what is known as 'Standard Habbie', basically a Scots form of verse, popularised by Burns but much older, and frequently utilised by the Ulster-Scots bards when writing in that tongue. It is interesting to note that the second extract from the poetry of Patrick Brontë is also written in this metre, though the language of the poem itself is standard English, unusually for this form. This and certain others of his earlier poems appear to show a poetic consciousness harking back to the literary milieu of the Ulster Scots poets.

IDENTIFICATIONS OF DEDICATIONS

Rev. B.

Rev Henry Boyd. Boyd was born in Co Tyrone, the son of
Charles Boyd, farmer. Educated in Trinity College, Dublin,
he was Vicar of Drumgath 1798 - 1809. Well-known as the
translator of Dante, he died in 1832.

W.B. Esq.

William Beers, the local proprietor, of Ballygorian and
Ballyward Lodge, Drumgooland (1760 - 1829). He built
Ballyward Lodge in 1811.

J.J. a brither rhymer

Possibly James Jackson of Emdale, who wrote rhyming
puzzles for the Belfast almanacs, though the poem
addresses him as 'Johnny'.

Rev. B.W.M.

Rev Benjamin Williams Mathias. He was born in Dublin,
the son of Benjamin Mathias, merchant, and was educated
in Trinity College. Curate of Drumballyroney 1801 - 1808,
he moved to Dublin and was Chaplain of the Bethesda
Chapel 1810 - 1841. He was a very popular preacher and
published theological works. He died in 1841.

Rev. D**** M****

Rev David McKee. Presbyterian minister of First Anaghlone
1804 - 1867. He also carried on a classical school, one of his
pupils being the novelist Capt Mayne Reid. He lived at
Ballynaskeagh. His daughter married the Rev Dr. Wright,
author of *The Brontës in Ireland*. He died in 1867.

Rev. I.P.

Rev Isaac Patrick, Presbyterian minister of Magherally
1756 - 1805. He died in 1814.

Rev. T***** M**** R***
Rev Thomas Mayne Reid. Presbyterian minister of
Drumgooland 1800 - 1852. His father was John Reid,
farmer, of Donacloney. His son was the novelist Capt
Mayne Reid. He was appointed Clerk of the Secession
Synod in 1827 and remained Joint Clerk of the General
Assembly from the union of the synods in 1840 until his
death in 1868.

T.J.T. Esq.
Probably Thomas J. Tighe, who was a magistrate in
Rathfriland in the 1850s. He died in 1860.

Rev. T.T.
Rev Thomas Tighe. Tighe was the son of William Tighe,
M.P., of Rosanna, Co Wicklow. He went to St John's
College, Cambridge. He was Vicar of Drumgooland 1778 -
1821, Vicar of Drumballyroney 1778 - 1821, and Rector of
Drumgooland 1787 - 1821. He married, in 1786, Eliza,
daughter of William Beers, of Ballygorian, Co. Down. He
died in 1821.

T.T. Esq.
Probably Thomas Trew, one of the subscribers.

SUBSCRIBERS' NAMES

A

Right Hon. Earl Annesley 4
James Arbuckle, Esq.
Hon Lady Sophia Arbuckle
Thomas Acton, Esq. 4
Mrs Acton
Miss Acton
Rev William Atthill, Fintona
Rev Isaac Allen, Willowbrook
Rev Mr Arnold, Warrenpoint
Charles Archbold, Esq.
Mr Joseph Abbott, Dublin
W.W. Arabin, Esq.
George Agnew, Esq. Moss Vale
Messrs. Gil. Adams, Rathfriland
John Adams, Ballybrick
Alexander Adams
John Adams, Jun.
John Atkins, Newry
William Alexander, Surgeon,
        Rathfriland
Captain Aljoe
Mrs Aljoe
Mrs Atkinson, Armagh
Messrs Archbold and Dugan 5
Mr Thomas Arnold, Ballynahinch
Mr Henry Atkinson, Belfast
Mr James Arnold, Ballymacasban
Mr Allen, Comber

B

Hon. B. Bouverie 4
William Brownlow, Esq.
Thomas Bligh, Esq.
John Blachford, Esq. 4

James Blackwood, Esq.
Rev R. Bagwell, Dean of Clogher
Rev James Brown, B.D.F. St.
        John's, Cambridge
Rev B. Bridge, F. St. Peter's
        Coll, Cambridge
Rev T. Beatty, Vicar General of
        Dromore
Rev James Brown, B.D.F. St. John's
        Coll. Cambridge
Rev H.E. Boyd, Preb. of Dromara
Oliver Burke, Esq. F.M. Town
William Beers, Esq.
Mrs Beers
Crane Brush, Esq.
Rev H. Boyd 5
Rev F. Burrowes, Seapatrick
John Boyd, Esq. Customhouse,
        Dublin
Mrs I. Boyd
Captain Boyd, R. South Down
        Militia
Rev E. Berwick
Mr James Barton, Bolton-street,
        Dublin
Miss Barnewall, French-street
Mr M.B.
John Birch, Esq. Lisburn st.
Mrs Birley, Blackburn, Lancashire
Miss Birley
Miss Jane Birley
Miss Mary Birley
Mrs Bower
Dr Bingham, Rosstrevor
Rev James Birch, Dromara
Mr M. Barr, Ballynahinch
Miss Barber, Tullyquilly

Mr He. Boyle, Rockmount
J.W.Bell, Esq.
Mrs Black, Stranmillis
Rev Charles Boyd, Clanduffe
Rev Dr Blacker
Rev J.L. Blacke
Miss Beers
Mr D. Boyd, Monisland
Miss Boyd
Mr Richard Bryans, Merchant,
       Newry
Master Francis Bryans
Mr James Bigham, Tullynasoo
John Barnes, Esq. Armagh
Messrs William Barnes, Ditto
Francis Bennet, Ditto
—— Burrowes
Miss Barnes, Armagh
Messrs Archer Bayly
M. Bodel, Dromore
John Blakeney, Ballynahinch
Robert Brennen, Belfast
Alexander Barr, Ditto
Robert Briggs, Ditto
Thomas Bell, Ditto
John Bellingham, Esq.
Sir James Bristow
Wm. Bateson, Esq. Orangefield
Rev George Birch, Comber
Mr Alan Bell, Crumlin
Hugh Bowden, Esq. Ballyward
Samuel Bell, Esq. Newry

C

His Grace Charles Lord
Archbishop of Cashel 4
Rt Hon Countess Clanwilliam 2
Right Hon Earl Clanwilliam
Right Hon Earl of Caledon

Right Hon Countess of Caledon
Hon Lady Anne Clements
Hon Lady Eliza Clements
Hon Lady Louisa Clements
Right Rev Lord Bishop of Clogher
Mrs Carleton, Green Park
Trevor Corry, Esq. 2
Smithson Corry, Esq. 2
Miss Corry
Rev Mr Campbell, Glastry
Richard Cardwell, Esq. Blackburn
Charles Christian, Esq.
Dawson Church, Esq.
Mrs Clarke, Rathmines 2
Mr George Clarke
Mrs Walter Crawford
Messrs Samuel Carothers,
          Ballynahinch
Thomas Carson, Ballyward
John Corbitt, Ditto
James Cinnamon, Leitrim
John Chirmside, Portaferry
T. Chreighton, Ditto
John Corbitt, Lisnacrevy
Chippendale Manchester
Samuel Corbitt, Tullynasoo
Patrick Cuningham, Belfast
William Christian, Rathfriland
Robert Carson, Monisland
William Cochran, Merchant,
       Newry
Rev Mr Cooke, Anacloan
Mr Patrick Cuningham, Drumca
Samuel Craige, Armagh
John Carry, Gracehill
Rev Dr Cupples, Lisburn
Mrs Coulter, Armagh
Messrs William Carroll, Belfast
John Cunningham, Ditto
Thomas Campbell, Ditto

John Crossley, Ditto
Edward Curteis, Esq. Glenburne
Mr William Clawson, Belfast
Hugh Crawford, Esq.
                Crawfordsburn
Mr Robert Cumming, Comber
Mr Samuel Crory, Lackan

D

Most Noble the Marquis of
                Downshire 10
Right Hon. Earl of Darnley
Right Rev Thomas (Late) Lord
        Bishop of Dromore 4
Right Rev John Lord Bishop of
        Dromore 4
Thomas Dowglass, Esq. Grace Hall
Rev Mr Davis, Chanc. of Dromore
Rev I. Dubourdieu, Anahilt
Rev C. Dalton, Kelvedon, Essex
Peter du Cane, Jun Esq.,
                Braxted Lodge
John Davison, Esq. Armagh
—— Drought, Esq.
Messrs Samuel Dobbin, Moira
Cornelius Douglass
John Doyle, Belfast
Clotworthy Dobbin
John Dodd, Ballynahinch
James Dalzell, Marlefield
Arthur Davison, Edengary
William Dillon, Lisburn
Mrs S. Dickson, Armagh
Leonard Dobbin, Esq. Ditto
Robert Douglass, Esq. Armagh
Mr James Dunn, Belfast
Rev Doctor Drummond,
                Mount Collier
Mr Stephen Daniel, Belfast

Rev Samuel Dickson, Bangor
Mr Robert Dunn, Dunore

E

Hon. and Right Rev Lord Bishop
        of Ferns 4
Isaac A. Eccles, Esq. Cronroe 2
Major Eccles
Mrs Earbery 4
Rev S. Edgar, Armagh
Mr John Edgar, Ditto

F

Rev James Fawcett, B.D. Norrisian
Professor of Divinity,
                Cambridge
Rev Robert Fiske, F. St. John's
                Cambridge
Rev Robert Fiske, A.M. Fulbourne
Rev Robert Fawcett, Armley,
                Yorkshire
John Fivey, Esq. Loughbrickland
James Freke, Esq.
Mrs J. Freke
Meredith Foxall, Esq. Newry
Mr Feilden, Witton
Mr W. Feilden, Ditto
Captain William Forrest, Jun.
                Warrenpoint
Mr Isaac Fleming

G

Right Hon Countess of Granard
Right Hon Earl of Glandore 4
Mr W.S. Guinnes
Robert Gibson, Drumalig
William Gibson, Ditto

Edward Gray, Warrenpoint
William Gilliland, Fishquarter
Robert Getty, Merchant, Dundalk
Matthew Gaskin, Seaforde
William Glenny, Esq. Newry
Mr John Gowdy, Surgeon,
           Castlewellan
Messrs Henry L. Gardner, Belfast
Robert P. Grimshaw, Ditto
Robert Getty, Ditto
Mrs Robert Galway, Comber
Joseph Garner, Esq
Miss Garner

H

Right Hon. Earl of Hardwicke,
           K.G.
Right Hon Countess of Hardwicke
Hon. Col. Howard
Rev T.W. Hornbuckle, F. St.
       John's Coll. Cambridge
Rev T. Heberden, Canon of
       Exeter
Roger Hall, Esq. Narrow Water
William Hoey, Esq
Chas. Hamilton, Esq. Hamwood
Mrs C. Hamilton
Mrs Hamilton, Lucan Lodge
Miss Hamilton
Alex. Hamilton, Esq
Mrs A. Hamilton
Mrs H. Hamilton, Hazle Bank
Rev Chas. Hamilton, Tullylish
Messrs. Hamilton and Townsend,
       Dublin
Mr S.L. Hamilton, Ballydown
Mr Geo. Hamilton
Dr Harty, Dublin
Mrs Harty
John Hornby, Esq. Blackburn

Mrs Hornby
Joseph Hornby, Esq. ditto
J.F. Hindle, Esq. ditto
Miss Holliday, Ballynahinch
Mr John Herron, ditto
Mr Hoey, Knutzden
James Hogg, Esq
Mrs Holmes
Mr Henston, Surgeon, Clough
Mr Robert Herron, Leitrim
Miss Hull
Miss M.J. Hull
Miss Eliza Harrison, Kelvedon
Messrs David Henderson, Newry
Maurice Haughey, ditto
John Haughey, Armagh
R. Harrington, ditto
Rev T.E. Higginson, Lisburn
Rev Edward Hamilton,
       Donaghadee
Mrs Hemsworth, Armagh
Major Hill, ditto
Messrs. Wm. Heuston,
       Drumadonald
Alexander Halliday, Terragory
Edward Hill, Belfast
Henry Holden, ditto
William Higginson, ditto
Rev Edward Hamilton,
       Donaghadee
Edward Hull, Esq. ditto
Mr Robt. Henry, Cullintrough
Mr Thos. Hart, Comber

I

Arthur Innis, Esq. Glen
John Ingrams, Esq. Allybrooke
Messrs James Ireland, Belfast
John Irwin, ditto

J

Hon Lady Caroline Jocelyn 2
Hon Lady Charlotte Jocelyn 2
Hon Lady Frances Jocelyn
Hon Lady Anne Jocelyn
Right Hon Lord Visct. Jocelyn
Rev Geo. Mc.D. Johnson
Hon Lady Anne Johnson
Rev Th. Jackson, B.D. F. St. John's
    Coll. Cambridge
Rev J. Jebb, Abington, Limerick
Mrs Jebb
Mr F. Johnson, Derryneall

K

Right Hon and Right Rev Lord
    Bishop of Kildare
John Keowen, Esq. Tollymore
Mrs Kelly 4
Messrs John Kelsey
Thos. Kerr, Shanaghan
John Kerr, Ballynahinch
Pat. Kelly, Dundalk
Dan. Kean, Rathfriland
John Kearns, Gransha
Henry Kidd, Armagh
John Kane, ditto
Hugh Kidd, ditto
J. Knowles, Belfast
Hugh Kennedy, Esq. Cultra

L

Right Hon Earl of Leitrim
Right Hon Countess of Leitrim
Hon Mrs Lindsay
Rev Rd. Littlehales, Lopham,
    Norfolk
J. Lindsay, Esq. Cork

Miss Cath. Leland
Miss Anne Leland
Chas Latouche, Esq.
Robert G. Leslie, Esq.
Michael Lacy, Esq.
John Lloyd, Esq. Gloster
Rev John Leslie
Rev S. Livingston, Portaferry
John Law, Esq.
Wm. Law, Esq.
Alex. Lowry, Esq.
Cap. Lindsay, Maghera
Mr James Lindsay, Ballygorian
Miss Lindsay, Ballyachian
Miss Ledsom, Rathmines
Mr Chas. Lewis, Kirkeel
Mr Sam. Law
Miss Ellen Lechey, Bailyborough
Messrs. Joseph Lavery,
    Ballymielrainy
Joseph Lee, Armagh
— Lindley, Armagh
Jos. Lemon, Donaghadee
Alex. Laughlin, Dunover
Mons. Le Pan

M

Right Hon Countess of
    Massareene 4
Right Hon Earl of Mexborough
Right Hon Countess of
    Mexborough
Right Hon Lord Visct. Midleton 8
Hon Lady Maria Meade
Hon John Meade, Lt. Col. 4.th 4
Hon and Rev. P. Meade,
    Archdeacon of Dromore 4
James M'Donnell, Esq. M.D.
    Belfast
Major Miller

Rev Andrew Millar, Lungs
John Corry Moutray, Esq.
    Favor-royal
Luke Magrath, Esq.
Michael Mills, Esq. 4
W.H. Mecredy, Esq. 4
Rev Bl. Mitchell
Rev Jas. Maffett, Maghera
Rev I. M'Cormick,
    Loughbrickland 4
Rev B.W. Mathias 4
Rev John M'Cleland, Ballynahinch
Rev D. Makee, Anacloan
Rev T. Makee, Castlewellan
Robert Mecredy, Esq
Henry M'Veagh, Esq
Maxwell M'Master, Esq.
Rev Wm. Moreland, Portaferry
James M'Key, Esq.
George M'Key, Esq.
Fitch Matthews, Esq.
Messrs John M'Calla, Rockvale
George M'Kee
Wm. M'Cleery, Jun.
Thos. M'Teer, Warrenpoint
Miss Moore, Derryoge
Rev Jos. M'Neilly, Rathfriland
Sam. Murphy, Esq. ditto
Miss Myers
Miss Isabella West M'Neill,
    Glasgow
Mr Alex. Mackey
Thomas Murray, Esq. 8
Lieut Mecredy, R.S.D. Militia
Messrs. John M'Murray, Gransha
Robt. M'Mullen, Ballybay
John Moffett, Drumdreenan
O. M'Mullan, Castlewellan
Wm. Magher, Esq.
Sam. Magher, Esq.

Rev D. Maxwell, Newtownards 2
Rev Geo. M'Cleland, Ahoghill 2
Messrs. Sam. M'Alister,
    Derrydrummuck
Sam. Morrison, Monisland
Robert Mollan, Newry
Robert M'Cune, ditto
John Morgan, Armagh
S. Maxwell, ditto
Edmund M'Ildowney, Ballycastle
Messrs. Wm. M'Comb, Belfast
John M'Cutcheon, ditto
Dan. Magenis, Armagh
Andrew Maziere, Esq.
Mrs J. Mee, Shantolly Glebe
Thos. M'William, Esq.
Wm. M'William, Esq.
Messrs. John Makee, Belfast
James M'Bride, Monisland
Rev John Mulligan, Moira
Messrs. John M'Adam, Belfast
Stephen Moreland, ditto
Robert M'Dowel, ditto
Alex. Moreland, ditto
J. Murray, Surgeon, ditto
Robert M'Kibbin, ditto
Robert M'Adam, ditto
Rev. Jos. M'Culloch, Gransha
Capt. M'Mahon
— Alexander
Messrs. Jas. M'Connel, Comber
Henry Murray, ditto
Thos. Martin, Newtownards
Wm. Moore, Newtownards
Miss Jane M'Connell, Comber
Miss Jane M'Kee, White Church
Miss Anne Maxwell, Ballywalter
Mr John M'Clenaghan, Jun.
    Belfast

N

Mrs Newell, King Hill
Messrs Nevill, Blackburn
John Neisbitt, Ballynaskeagh
Thos. Nicholson, Kirkeel
W.B. Neilson, Belfast
Wm. Newsam, ditto

O

Hon Lady Catherine O'Donnell
Rev H. Ormsby
Lieut O'Neil, Castlewellan
Miss O'Neil
Michael O'Loughlan, Esq.
Messrs. Alex. Orr, Belfast
Daniel O'Neill, Warrenpoint
Thomas O'Neill, Belfast
John Orr, Esq.

P

Right Hon Lord Visc. Pollington
Right Hon Lady Viscts. Pollington
Hon Lady Elizabeth Pratt
Nicholas Price, Esq.
Hon Lady Sarah Price
Mrs Porter, Clogher
Sir Isaac Pennington, Regius
        Professor of Physic,
        Cambridge
Rev John Phillips, D.D. Berstead,
        Sussex
Thomas Pearson, F. St. Peter's
        Coll. Cambridge
George Palmer, Esq,
        French-street, Dublin
George Palmer, Jun. Esq.
Richard Palmer, Esq.

Mrs Palmer
Miss Palmer
Rev Robert Porter, Clough
Rev Robert L. Porter, Portnorris
Rev James Porter, Drumlee 5
Messrs Alexander Porter,
                Drumadonald
Samuel Porter, Monisland
Robert Porter, ditto
George Paxton, Ballynahinch
Miss Pidgeon, Rathmines
Messrs Joseph Paterson
John Parke, Rathfriland
Hamilton Potter, Killinchy
Mrs A. Prentice, Armagh
Miss S. Prentice, ditto
Messrs Edward Porter, Belfast
Isaac Patton, ditto
Robert Patterson, ditto
John Porter, ditto
Capt. Pollock, Portaferry
Mr Joseph Penny, Ardaghy

Q

Messrs Thomas Quaile, Down
Arthur Quin, Belfast

R

Right Hon Earl of Roden
Right Hon Countess of Roden
John L. Reilly, Esq.
John Rankin, Esq. M.D.
Col. Robert Ross, 20th. Regt.
Solomon Richards, Esq. 2
Robert Richards Esq.
Rev Dr Russell, Ashbrook
Rev Thomas Ross, Rostrevor
Rev T.M. Reid, Closkelt

Rev John Rogers, Glasker
S.I. Ryan, Esq. Clonmel
James Mervyn Richardson, Esq.
    Castle Hill
Mrs Reid, White Abbey
Messrs James Rowan, Surgeon,
    Belfast
James Rea, Derryneill
John Roberts, Woodburn
John Rea, Belfast
Lewis Reford, ditto
Alexander Robinson, ditto
William Ralph, Comber
William Robison, ditto

S

Right Hon. Earl Spencer 4
William Smyth, Esq. Professor of
    Modern History,
    Cambridge
Rev T. Sheepshanks, Wimpole
William Sheepshanks, Esq. Trin.
    Coll. Cambridge
Mrs Stewart, Lakefield
Miss Stewart
Miss S. Stewart
John Stewart, Esq. Wilmont
Mrs Stewart, Wilmont
Thomas Stewart, Esq.
William Sharman, Esq.
Aaron Seymour, Esq.
James Shaw, Esq. Kircubbin
William Scott, Esq. Rathfriland
Thomas Scott, Esq. ditto
Mrs Symes 2
Miss Marianne Symes 2
Rev Dr Stack, Kilskeery
Rev Dr Story, Corick
Rev T. Starkie, Blackburn

Rev M. Sandys, Waltrim 2
Mrs Sandys 2
Rev W. Smyth, Liverpool 2
Miss Isabella Stouppe
Mrs Stephenson, Hillsborough
Messrs. John Service, Belfast
Thomas Simpson, Moira
John Shaw
— Spellance
John Smyth, Ballynahinch
Samuel Smyth, ditto
James Scott, ditto
Capt. Sheals, Warrenpoint
Messrs James Shaw, Portaferry
William Swan, Lisnacrevy
Wm. Swan, Gralloughgreenan
Thomas Small, Drumca
Matthew Spires, Surgeon,
    Monisland
John Scott, Rathfriland
James Stuart, Esq. Newry
Mr Wilson Sproule, Armagh
Robert Stephens, Esq. ditto
Mrs Thos. Simpson, ditto
John Simpson, Esq. M.D. ditto
Messrs. Thomas Simpson, Belfast
John Galt Smith, ditto
Cortland Skinner, Esq. ditto
Mr Robert Slattery, Comber

T

Rev Ralph Tatham, B.D. Public
    Orator of the University
    of Cambridge
Rev Archdeacon Trail
William Tighe, Esq. 4
Henry Tighe, Esq. 4
Captain Tighe, R.S.D. Militia 5
Rev Dr Thorpe

Rev Thomas Tate, Rathfriland
H.W. Tennent, Esq. Belfast
Thomas Trew, Esq
S. Thompson, M.D. Belfast
Rev Mr Thompson, ditto
Mr James Todd, Rathfriland
Mrs Thompson
Messrs. James Todd,
              Ballynaskeagh
James Turner, Warrenpoint
Robert Telfair, Belfast

V

Rev Thomas Vensey, F. St. Peter'
          Coll. Cambridge

W

Right Hon Colonel R. Ward, 10
Hon Miss Harriet Ward
Lieutenant Colonel J.R. Ward,
         27th. Regiment 2
Captain M.E. Ward, R.S.D.M. 2
Rev James Wood, President of St.
         John's College,
         Cambridge
Luke White, Esq.
H.S. Willock, Esq.
James Wallace, Esq. Rockmount
Mrs Wilson, Maryville
Rev W.B. Whitfield, F. St. John's
       College, Cambridge
Mrs Williams
Rev Holt Waring, Waringstown 4
Rev J. Wallace, Braxted
Rev Richard Wolseley,
           Loughinisland
Rev Henry Wolseley, St. Field
Rev Charles Wolseley

Mrs Waring, Bell Hill
Richard Waring, Esq. Armagh
Mrs Whittington, Armagh
Mr Alexander Wilkinson, Newry
James Wallace, Esq. Down
Mrs J. Wallace
Mr John Williamson, Drumca
John Wilson, Anahinchisc
Rev David Whyte, Ballee
Mr John Wallace, Belfast
Mr John Woodside, ditto
Robert Wallace, Esq.

Y

Hon Lady Elizabeth Margaret
         Yorke
Hon Lady Caroline Harriot Yorke

THE AUTHOR'S DEDICATION
TO
THE RIGHT HON. EARL OF MOIRA

MY LORD,

AS some weak harmless hame-spun wretch,
Unfit to cope wi' e'en his match,
Yet sees assembling crowds - in strife
Which o' them first will take his life,
Looks round him for some generous friend
That may his innocence defend:

Now, such an one as this he sees -
But though his very vitals freeze
At thoughts of dire approaching blows,
And though his wish'd for help he knows
To be intent on generous deeds,
Yet fears to ask what most he needs:
So I, in long suspence have stood,
Aw'd by the snarling Critic brood,
Elate with scientific pride;
But now since MOIRA joins my side,
Protected by that sheltering shield,
I'll brave the fiercest on the field,
Repeating still, where e'er I go -
If HE say aye, who dare say no.

THE AUTHOR'S PREFACE

READER,

SINCE ye hae gie'n your five an' fi'ppence,
For this bit Beuk, that's no worth tippence;
Anither page or twa o' paper,
Wad mak it aye leuk something cheaper;
At least mak mair o't for the money -
Say, shall I then impose't upon ye?
'Yes, if ye please, and after a'
'Five shillin' will be thrown awa.
'But stop - I think I have enough,
'I b'live owre muckle o' sic stuff;
'Yet, neither here nor there a leaf is,
'Come, gie's it in the way o' preface.

First then, I naething write by rule,
For o' the knowledge taught at school
Mine was a very scanty share,
I only learn'd the letters there:
Yet, by degrees, wi' tentie head,
At leisure hours I came to read;
And thus, by bit an' bit I grew
That I could write a little too,
A willin' mind a deal can do.

And secondly, plain truth to tell,
I made my sangs to please my sel',
My dearest worthy frien's, and ithers
No' just sae dear, but rhymin' brithers
To whom, just as they are, I sent them,
But never for the public meant them.

And thirdly, in the style appears
The accent o' my early years,
Which is nor Scotch nor English either,
But part o' baith mix'd up thegither:
Yet its the sort my neighbours use,
Wha think shoon prettier far than shoes.

But fourthly, for I'm keen to close -
'Do - do - ye'll say - an' do't in prose
'For flesh an' bluid can bear nae langer,
'This doggerel sang a saint would anger.'
Content am I, and for the Muse,
I'm sure she's glad to hear the news.

Then fourthly, as I said before,
(But whist - for I must rhyme no more)

If I be guilty of plagerism, it is only where I
am unable to distinguish between the imagination
and memory.

TO THE REVEREND T. T. PARSON'S HILL

REVEREND SIR,

I WOULD be laith,
Your honour in the least to skaith,
Tho' I repining bend beneath
　　The want of rare things;
But ye hae wealth and honour baith
　　An' mony mair things.

Few persons can wi' you compare
In what the great and worthy share,
Yet och! if I had but the lear
　　That ye hae gotten,
I would not value a' your gear
　　An eyeless button.

For then I could baith write and spell,
An' speak, and leuk, grammatical,
An' would sic rhyming blethers tell
　　'Tween truth and lies,
As Maister Dick, or e'en yoursel',
　　Might may-be please.

But let us first our tale declare:
Ae Sunday night to banish care,
I to your dwelling-house repair,
　　Wi' right guid will,
An' if it was for sake o' prayer
　　That's better still.

I entered in your parlour door,
And as I stalked owre the floor,
I saw - but sic a sight before
　　I ne'er had seen,
A thousand beuks I'm sure, and more,
　　Surpriz'd my een.

Thought I - if e'er it be my lot
To be a prisoner - here's the spot
Of a' the world I would have got
    To be my jail,
Here heart-corroding care should not
    My soul assail:

I could spen' mony a cheerfu' summer
To crack wi' Virgil, Pope, an' Homer,
It raises in my brain a rumour
    To hear them talk'd o',
But waes my heart - what fits my humour
    I'm often baulk'd o';

While I survey'd this pompous pile,
O' beuks in order, rank and file,
This sweet reflection made me smile
    He's condescendin',
An' will, perhaps, for a short while
    Vouchsafe to lend ane.

Amang the rest that me attracts
There's ane, of which I hear great cracks,
An' that's the "Elegant Extracts,"
    So, if ye hae it,
Your humble Rhymer, Sir, expects,
    Or hopes ye'll gie it.

I'll read as much o't as I can,
An' what I canna read - maun stan',
I'll keep it clean wi' carefu' han',
    Nor tear nor burn it,
An' ony time that you deman',
    I will return it.

Now gin your Reverence would please
To grant me this but twa-three days,
I'll teach the lanely burns and braes
    The heights an' hollows,
To join wi' me in Scottish lays,
    An' sing as follows:

Oh! may your Reverence be blest
Wi' health, an' strength, an' peace, an' rest;
An' may contention ne'er infest
    Your social meetings,
But mutual love be aye exprest
    In kindly greetings;

An' may ye lang enjoy wi' credit,
The douse black gown, for weel ye set it,
May nane ye wish weel e'er be fretit,
    I pray most fervent,
For want of lear, or means to get it
    As is your servant,

HUGH PORTER
    July, 1799.

TO THE REVEREND T.T. PARSON'S HILL

I THANK ye, Sir, for your "Extracts,"
    As gratefully as can be,
An' till the golden bowl it brakes
    What ance I say I'll stan' by,
Though I'm owre apt mysel' to vex,
    I'm sometimes blythe as brandy,
Sometimes I read, an' gather cracks
    Frae Larry's "Tristram Shandy".

Sometimes I rake alang a rill,
    And ither times I stan' there,
Sometimes I think on Parson's Hill,
    But mair upon the Man there,
Wha first indulg'd my tinklin skill
    An' took me by the han' there,
An' ca'd me frien' wi' free guid will
    An' frien'ship firm I fan' there.

I own I dreamed o' sma' success,
    Before I was acquainted
Wi' you or your true nobleness,
    Yet my request was granted,
I got, I frankly maun confess
    The very thing I wanted,
I sought nae mair - I got nae less,
    Right suddenly ye sent it.

For loss o' glory, or o' gear,
    I stan' in little danger,
For to the twa I'll frankly swear
    I'm still a down-right stranger;
Nae wonner he wad fortune fear
    That never friendly finds her,
For she's or deaf, or winna hear,
    Or partial passion blinds her.

If I had by some lucky lot,
 Been born in sic a station,
Whare I might timeously hae got
 A mod'rate education,
And some sequester'd lonely cot
 Wi' beuks o' information -
Say, Rector, would I've had or not
 A sweeter situation.

Nae doubt ye'll say, P*****, poor deil,
 For some self en's is clatt'rin',
But aiblins time might gar you feel
 I hae nae thought o' flatt'rin',
When ilka lassie at her wheel,
 An' ilka aged matron,
Shall sing, the Reverend Rector chiel
 Is now the Rhymer's Patron.

Sud fortune in a fit o' wrath
 This speech to you deliver,
'Wi' P*****, Sir, your gear an' graith,
 'Ye maun exchange for ever,'
I doubt your honour wad be laith
 To knuckle to the niffer;
Yet if the skin were aff us baith
 There wad be little differ.

'Your pardon, Sir, for makin' free,
 I own that I hae said ill,
But yet I hope ye will forgie
 My random written schedule:
For manners ye may plainly see
 I learn'd upon the treadle,
An' for my state, my stars an' me
 Hae squabbl'd frae the cradle.

If my unruly muse has been
 Owre forward, I'll correct her,
An' just before your Reverend een,
 Her noddle, here I'll fracture,

For sure the like was never seen
    By the most sage inspector:
A frien'liness commenced between
    A Rhymer and a Rector.

Sud ill fate 'mang my barmy brain,
    I'll never swing for swervin',
For o' a' ye possess - in plain
    Me thinks ye're weel deservin';
A flattrin' lie I winna feign,
    Tho' I sud die in starvin',
What I was still, I still remain,
    Your rhymin' crack-skull servan',

HUGH PORTER.
    September, 1799.

TO REVEREND T.T.
AFTER AN ABSENCE OF SOME WEEKS

COME my auld hide-bound Muse, draw near,
An' welcome hame our Maister dear,
For he it seems, has na been here
    This month an' mair;
We'll then salute him wi' this cheer,
    Ye're welcome, Sir.

How com'st, my Muse, ye take the gaet
At sic a sober cauld-rife rate,
Resume your wonted, wished-for state,
    An' void o' care,
Let ev'ry stanza terminate,
    Ye're welcome, Sir.

To tell the truth unfeignedly -
Indeed my heart was somewhat wae
To hear that Master Richard lay
    Baith sick an' sair;
But since he's weel - again I say,
    Ye're welcome, Sir.

Ye hae been i' the royal city,
Amang the wealthy an' the witty,
An' far-fetch'd compliments an' pretty,
    Are plenty there;
But this is just a hame-spun ditty, -
    Ye're welcome, Sir.

I need na talk about your entry
Amang the noble Dublin gentry,
 'Twad keep me scribbling near a cent'ry,
    This to declare;
I'll just speak for my native country,
    Ye're welcome, Sir.

God save the Rector, is a sang
That's learn'd long-syne - dear kens how lang
To greet your lugs as by ye gang;
    Whilst I prepare,
To give the echo to the thrang,
    Ye're welcome, Sir.

I think, indeed, without a lie,
There's nane of any ae degree
But what will strive to join with me,
    Wi' heart sincere;
Nobles, and Squires, and Peasantry,
    Ye're welcome, Sir.

While some, wi' slee an' cannie art
Do sing to please ye - for my part,
It was your safe return that gart
    My Musie stir,
An' tune this greeting frae the heart,
    Ye're welcome, Sir.

At times, when I the Muse invoke
I just steal out frae 'mang the folk;
Ye ken the bush beside the rock,
    I trow 'twas there,
By her directed, thus I spoke,
    "Ye're welcome, Sir."

Here often in the blaze of bliss,
I meet with the Parnassian Miss,
An' there I toy, and court, an' kiss,
    An' crack wi' her;
An, there she bid me scribble this,
    Ye're welcome, Sir.

I'll ne'er forget the sweet wee whiles,
I spend wi' her 'mang woodie wilds,
Her pretty gleesome dainty smiles
    I'll aye revere;
This oft the tardie time beguiles,
    Ye're welcome, Sir.

I make na this rhyming report
For ony ends, but just for sport;
I'll min' December twenty-fort,
    For ever mair;
But to make a long story short,
    Ye're welcome, Sir.

That Gude may bless you a' your days,
An' grant you meat, an' drink, and claes,
An' aye defend you frae your faes,
    Is P*****'s prayer;
An' now to read your Bardie's lays,
    You're welcome, Sir.

26 December 1802.

ON THE ECLIPSE OF THE SUN, 11 FEBRUARY, 1804

O! BUT the fountain-head o' day
    Shines bright this morn,
The south-east side o' many a brae
    His beams adorn;
An' yet lang-headed bodies hae
    Baith said and sworn,
E'er ye send forth your noon-tide ray,
    Ye'll be folorn.

Oh! but it is a pity ye
    Sud thole disgrace,
Or that in masquerade sud be
    Sae fair a face;-
Methinks that ither orbs to thee
    Sud a' gie place,
An' let you always tak' and gie
    Your will o' space.

Fy on ye, moon, they say its you
    That does this deed,
That fills the kintra, thro' an' thro'
    Wi' fellon dread;
Our tim'rous spirits to subdue
    Ye strive to cleed
His life invigoratin' hue
    In mournin' weed.

Come o' us wretches here what will,
    Ye dinna care,
Gin ye by wiles can keep yoursel
    Frae blot and scare;
In brightness, ye would fain excel
    A' orbs that are,
But bide some twa-three months, we'll tell
    What's then your share.

Within this while as mickle skaith
    Yoursel has fan',
Your visage was as dark as death,
    Whar' ye did stan';
To rip auld sairs, I wad be laith
    To tak' in han',
But ye hae shawn sae mickle wrath,
    Owre a' the lan'.

Ye ought to be content to shine
    In your ain sphere,
An' no to make us mortals dwine
    In darkness here;
Since ye in the dependant line,
    Get a' your gear,
It fits ye weel, and a' your kin'
    To keep the rear.

Ye min' me o' ambitious man
    That's never right,
Gin ony ither chap be fan'
    To shine mair bright;
He'll mak' his merits, if he can,
    As dark as night,
That foremost, he himsel' may stan'
    In glorious light.

But frae this time, I warn ye fairly,
    To keep awa
Frae aff his suburbs, late and early,
    A mile or twa;
For pay your debt, you'll blink but barely
    Aboon the ba';
Your fickle face will leuk but queerly,
    An' far frae braw.

Whene'er yon glorious globe is set,
    Then wear the crown;
But at his rise, what power ye get
    Ye maun lay down;
Suppose alternately ye're let
    Blink there aboon,
I hope, my lass, ye'll no' forget
    Ye're but a Moon!

TO THE REVEREND T.T.

WE talk o' ha'in' hoards o' treasure,
That we may live a life o' leisure,
An' pass our days in peace an' pleasure,
    Void o' vexation;
But seldom do we min' to measure
    Their short duration.

E'en frien'ship, that baith was, and is,
Oft times a pure an' lastin' bliss,
Takes wings like wealth, an' wi' a biz,
    Bounds quite away;
I saw a noble proof o' this
    The ither day:

A sorry heart I had, to spy
Your Reverence ride the door cheek by,
An' no' to tell the reason why
    I was forgotten;
Before I'm sick, I see that I
    Am dead an' rotten.

Better to never be respected,
Than afterwards to be rejected,
For instantly we're a' infected,
    Heart, head, an' han';
Much war we could na' be afflicted
    By mortal man.

'Mang mis'ry's posts, whar I did sit,
My tongue took sic a faltrin' fit,
I thought the wee remains o' wit
    I had, was quat me;
Most Noble Rector, what is it
    That ails ye at me!

I did na want ye to come in,
Nor much to mind my mither's sin,
Yet ye might said, is sic na ane
    Alive or dead;
But like a man to save his skin
    Ye fled wi' speed.

Weel, since my pass-time's at an en',
I'll spill my ink an' burn my pen,
For wha amang the sons o' men
    Will ever min' me?
Since Rev'rend T****, my firmest frien',
    Has now resign'd me.

How joyfu' was my heart, ere while,
When ye wad meet me wi' a smile,
Ye'd first shake han's, in kindly stile,
    An' then hae cracked
As lang as ane could gane a mile
    Ye wad na slacked.

'Mang ither things, ye whiles wad say,
What way comes on the Muse the day?
Is she dung dumb, or what's the lay
    That's now her care?
Oh! are these glorious scenes away
    For ever mair?

But gin they be, I canna men' it,
Tho' deep in darkness, here I pen it,
The deafest lug ye hae shall ken it,
    Come next what will;
Therefore, I vow to GEORGE, I'll sen' it
    To Parson's Hill.

August, 1804.

TO DISAPPOINTMENT

O THOU! on mischief ever bent,
As far contemn'd, as weel ye're kent;
Few fellows will the loss lament,
    When Grumphie gets ye;
It seems ye hae been born in lent,
    For a' flesh hates ye.

And O! that ye had never yet
Been born, to keep my heart sae het,
Or had I been endow'd wi' wit
    To keep far frae ye;
For sure on earth, there's nane less fit
    To wingle wi' ye.

O happy ye! wha daily drudge
Thro' dirt an' dung, without a grudge,
Nor hope, nor fear, can e'er dislodge
    Your sluggish pace;
As deaf to honour, on ye trudge,
    As to disgrace.

Ye miserable, happy wretches,
Nae canker on your conscience catches -
Nae sic repose the thinker thatches
    Frae fear or fright;
But he or weeps, perhaps, or watches
    The live-lang night.

Ye're hale an' healthie now, an' therefore
Nae matter what comes next, or wherefore,
What crams your kits, is a' ye care for
    To taste or touch;
An' what we can be wantin' mair for,
    Ye marvel much.

Weel, happy be, ye peacefu' pack ye,
Happy as blockishness can mak' ye,
An' may vexation ne'er owertak' ye,
    To gar ye grane,
Nor blasted hopes, like mine, distract ye,
    Amen, amen.

TO REVEREND B.W.M.

DEAR REVEREND BEN,

I'm tauld you mean
    To be nae mair amang us,
A new addition to the train
    Of ills, that daily thrang us.

This hunted me away yestreen
    To Parson's Hill, right speedie,
That I for ance might feast my een
    On you, and your fair lady.

But lugs, forsooth, as well as een,
    Were bravely entertained,
And a' my secrets, leigh an' clean,
    Were openly explained;

This het my heart, tho' it was caul',
    An' hard as flint, an' harder,
Whare I stood trembling in the hall,
    An' durst na mint nae farder.

I sigh'd, an' said wi' little din,
    (The crystal tears they fell tho'),
Be wi' the time I wad been in,
    An' sitting at his elbow.

But yet, his Reverence does na' stick
    His blessing for to gie us,
To strengthen us anent auld Nick,
    Now when he's gaen to lea' us.

Had fortune in the least thee wrang'd,
    It wad been grun' for grumblin',
But lumps of dainty luck she whang'd,
    And toss'd them to you tumblin'.

So that what lease o' life was gi'en
    By fate, ye might hae spent it
Wi' Reverend T****, the man, the frien',
    An' dously been contented.

For had I fifty thousand pun'
    A year, o' ready money,
An' life as lang as Enoch's son,
    I'd seek nae ither cronie.

But here I'm buried up alive,
    Wi' crowds o' cares contendin',
Trampled beneath a hatefu' hive
    O' wretches, unbefriendin';

Whar pleasure never gies a blink
    On saul or body either;
An' black potatoes, a' the link
    That hauds the twa thegither.

So here I sit, misfortune's bairn,
    Lamentin', unlamented,
Exertin' a' my powers to learn -
    Frien'less, to be contented.

But whether ye or stay, or go,
    May nae sic ills betide ye,
An' round you aye, may pleasures flow,
    An' round your bonny bridie.

Wi' saut tears tricklin' frae may een,
    My last adieu I gie ye -
Fareweel my ever-honoured frien',
    May a' that's gude be wi' ye.

21st October, 1805.

A SONG ON MARRIAGE

THE day is come, my bonny bride,
　　That ye're my ain, and a' that,
Till death, we maun thegither bide:
　　They say, it is the law that,
　　The law that, the law that -
　　It is an unco law that,
The knot that tyes for life, it is
　　A knot that winna draw, that.

Weel, since it's sae, we'll n'er complain,
　　Nor ban our stars, an' a' that,
When love and friendship form the chain,
　　It never gies a ga' that,
　　For a' that, an' a' that,
　　Our kin'red sauls, an' a' that,
　　Are baith now souther'd up in ane -
　　It's love without a flaw, that.

There are o' ilka ae degree,
　　Would curse our state, an' a' that,
Wha wadna toil to plant the tree,
　　Would pou the fruit for a' that,
　　For a' that, an' a' that,
　　They're like the Cat, an' a' that,
　　"That wadna wat her fit" for fish,
　　But yet wad eat, for a' that.

They'll swear wi' love, they're like to dee,
　　But wait a wee, for a' that;
Gie them their will, they'll may be see,
　　They're no' as ill as a' that,
　　For a' that, an' a' that,
　　They'll deel, an' damn, an' a' that,
　　To ruin some poor orphan thing
　　That's no' awar o' a' that.

They'll grunt, an' grane, an' greet, an' glower,
    An' plot, an' scheme, an' a' that,
Their chastity to riot owre,
    Then fare ye weel, for a' that,
    For a' that, an' a' that,
    It's lang owre late, for a' that,
    To speak about a wadin' day,
    Gude faith, they'll keep awa' that.

But let them keek their heart within,
    When life's weel worn, an' a' that
An' there they'll find a sting behin',
    Will wound their peace for a' that,
    For a' that, an' a' that,
    Tho' they repent, an' a' that,
    Wi' bitter tears, an' sorry hearts,
    It winna sair for a' that.

But we, each ither's hearts shall keep
    Frae care, an' woe, an' a' that -
Tho' some may think we're ty'd like sheep,
    They're far mista'en, for a' that,
    For a' that, an' a' that;
    We're no' sae bun' as a' that:
    The ban's are sweet - when love's the law
    Its no' like ban's ava, that.

We'll steal thro' life, unknown to time,
    In innocence, an' a' that,
An' if we live without a crime,
    'Twill mak' us dee right braw, that,
    For a' that, an' a' that,
    There is a place an' a' that,
    Prepar'd for sic aboon the lift -
    The realms of bliss, they ca' that.

Sud death, each ither part us frae,
    There's comfort here for a' that;
Full on the verge of perfect day,
    We'll meet again, for a' that,
    For a' that, an' a' that;-
    If ye maun flit, an' a' that,
    Ye Mammonites, an' quat your cash,
    'Twill drive your wits awa, that.

THE BARD

BEHOLD the rustic Bard, O ye!
Wha' fortune, frownin', seldom see,
  Wha's coffers daily swell,
See pale-fac'd Age, an' Want arise,
An' daring dance before his eyes,
  Meager an' mirk as hell;
Thus hector'd, half his face appears
  In rigs an' sheughs already,
Which mak' him aulder than his years,
  An' aulder than his daddie;
    His sun how its run now,
    Far west, ere he's awar',
    Now dead is, an' fled his
    Meridian summer star.

Whan Winter storms, he stan's aghast,
To hear the desolatin' blast,
  Loud thund'rin' thro' the trees,
Which, like himsel', are leafless left,
Direct before the drivin' drift,
    To bear each bitter breeze;
    Nor is he free frae this assail,
    Within his crazy biggin;
    For even there, the pond'rous hail,
    Can thump him thro' the riggin';
    Yet there he, can share free
    Contentment, in a sense,
    For a' we're to ca' gear,
    He has it, but the pence.

If in a snawie winter night,
Ye watch the workin's o' the wight,
    Ye'll marvel what he's meanin',
Whar he sits nested i' the neuk,
Whiles blinkin', may be, on a beuk,
    Whiles on his elbow leanin',
Whiles whan a tunefu' notion comes,
    He's scribblin' wi' his pen;
Anon he flings it by, an' hums
    O' Shakespeare, king of men!
    Tears thick now, an' quick how
    They canter frae his een,
    Then sad-like, an' mad-like,
    He'll ban his stars in teen.

An' then, if crosses should him crush,
Or trains o' troubles on him rush,
    In a promiscuous thrang,
(For sic, nae strangers are to him),
He'll either hail them wi' a hymn,
    Or sooth them wi' a sang;
Or should his daily visitant *
    About his pillow prance,
An' there, in frightful form, present
    Her iron countenance,
    To smother, an' bother
    The melancholy croon,
    A sonnet, upon it,
    He'll mutter to the Moon.

* Misfortune

Then at the summer's sweet return,
Low by the brink o' some bit burn,
    Or on some grassy brae,
Reclin'd he lies, wi' up-turned ear,
And een half steek'd, intent to hear
    The lark's melodious lay;
In this delirium, deep I ween,
    Full monie a day he spen's,
Till gray-ey'd glomin' shut the scene
    Upon him, ere he kens;
    His heart then, will start when
    He hears the wakerife rail;
    Devotion's emotions,
    O'er all his pow'rs prevail.

Then he can sit nae longer still,
But up he gets, an' roun' the hill
    He steps sedately slow,
Straight to the weel-kent creek he hies,
While trains of bright ideas rise
    With many a grateful glow,
There prostrate falls - but O! what tongue,
    What language could declare,
What Cowper, Milton, or what Young,
    Could paint his powerful prayer?
    Then peaceful, an' graceful,
    Frae 'mang the blossom'd broom,
    He danders, an' wanders
    Towards his little home.

Thus spends the peaceful Bard his days,
With gratitude's refulgent rays
      Bright beaming in his breast,
Till Morpheus, ever friendly, brings
Sweet solace on his downy wings,
      An' lulls him into rest;
Then streekit on his strawy bed,
      He lies, an' sleeps as soun'
As royal *Geordie* ever did
      Upon his bed of down:
      A stranger to danger,
      An' fear of foreign force -
      No traitor lies wait, for
      To drain an empty purse.

O ye! wha bask in Fortune's ray,
An' row in rowth, frae day to day,
      Wha's path-way, pleasure paves;
How (shame upon ye), can ye stan'
An' heap preferment on a clan
      O' saucy, senseless knaves?
An' frien'less leave the simple Bard
      Amang the rustic boors,
And say his palate's no prepar'd
      For dainty bits like yours;
      For nature, the creature
      Has form'd plebeian, rude -
      Not so, we - for lo! we
      Are noble, great, an' good.

Weel, weel, to let the contest be,
Ye're as ye are, and so is he,
    An' that's nae great affair;
Tho' tramp'd beneath your pow'rful paws,
He has an honest heart, whereas -
    But I dare say nae mair,
Because I ken, he hasna cash
    To qualify his pouch,
Or else, aneath your tinkler snash,
    He wadna hae to crouch;
    Yet honour, her banner
    Might wave aboon his brow,
    An' lead him, to freedom,
    Tho' he's your vassal now.

But be that matter how it will,
He has a treble comfort still,
    That cheers him now an' then,
That is, at death, his cares will quat,
That thoughts are free through life, an' that
    His thoughts ye dinna ken:
His daily hope's your daily fear,
    His pleasure is your pain;
What least ye doat on, is his gear;
    What beets his bliss, your bane;
    Ye're bad baith, an' mad baith,
    An' sae'l be seen upon ye -
    Gude men' ye, an' sen' ye
    Mair wit, an' me mair money.

ON SEEING HIS NAME IN ROBINSON'S BOOK OF POEMS, WITH "ESQ." ADDED TO IT

MY up-start brethren, ane an' a',
Frae Dingle down to Derry wa',
Say, if ye ever heard or saw
    A thing sae queer,
As next to naebody ava
    Become a Squire.

Ere now, ye scarce wad met my match,
Suppose ye had been set to watch,
Or clad wi' patch on tap o' patch,
    Or buttock bare -
But now, the despicable wretch
    Is grown a Squire.

Whare drugget used to scrape my skin,
Now holland sheets, I'll row me in,
Instead o' brogues as hard as tin,
    I'll hae a pair
At least - a boot for ilka shin,
    Since I'm a Squire.

O, ROBINSON! may laurel green
Aye blooming on thy brow be seen,
And may nae crabbed critic, keen,
    Thy fame besmear;
But for thy bays, I ne'er had been
    Created Squire.

Now, at a vast prodigious rate
I'll scale the steepest steps of state,
There sit secure, and wink at fate,
    An' carpin' care;
Thanks to the generous and great,
    I'm now a Squire.

For me, the base-born beggar train
May pine, oppress'd wi' grief and pain,
For tho' I'm great, my greatness nane
    Shall ever share;
See, there its printed, pat an' plain,
    That I'm a Squire.

Nor age, nor want, to me need moan,
For a' sic scoundrels I disown -
Silence, I'll say, base vagabon',
    What brought ye there?
Perdition seize ye, wretch begone,
    Sure I'm a Squire.

An' he that disna quick retreat,
I'll tramp beneath my noble feet,
Oh! but I'll gar him groan an' greet,
    Or else forbear,
To mention money, milk, or meat;
    Yes, I'm a Squire.

Thus will I manage day by day
And haud the grip o' what I hae,
So by sic means, I may be, may
    Make mickle mair,
And force the folk, at length, to say
    Most noble Squire.

Then, whan I'll see the wretches stan'
Before me tremblin', hat in han'
O! I'll be big, an' great, an' gran',
    An' fat an' fair;
I question if in a' the lan'
    There's sic a Squire.

And if my expectation hit,
And I thrive on, I'll shortly sit
A royal - noble - what is it?
    An Emperor;
Preserve us! was there ever yet
    Sae great a Squire!

THE MUSE DISMISSED

BE hush'd my Muse, ye ken the morn
Begins the shearing o' the corn,
Whar knuckles monie a risk maun run,
An' monie a trophy's lost an' won,
Whar sturdy boys, wi' might an' main
Shall camp, till wrists an' thumbs they strain,
While pithless, pantin' wi' the heat,
They bathe their weazen'd pelts in sweat
To gain a sprig o' fading fame,
Before they taste the dear-bought cream -
But bide ye there, my pens an' papers,
For I maun up, an' to my scrapers -
Yet, min' my lass - ye maun return
The very night we cut the Churn.

THE MUSE RETURNS

TISANDER   GUID morrow to ye, honest woman,
Are ye gaun to, or are ye commin'
Frae *Hafiz, Robinson*, or *Drummon'*,
     Your famous friend?
Or is it *Boyd's* resistless summon,
     Ye now attend?

MUSE   Na, na, an humble course I steer,
For ane *Tisander*, now I spier:
A very vague, that's void, I hear
     O' shame and sense -
A haveril fellow; - am I near
     His residence?

TISANDER   See there, direct before your een,
The creature's cottage may be seen;
And there's the burn an' slopin' green,
     His pastime place;
And here's the wight himsel', I ween
     Before your face.

MUSE   Forgie me, Sir, I didna know ye;
Far mair respect, I own, I owe ye;
Tune up your harp, and I'll bestow ye
     A lyric string,
Besides, a knack, which whon I'll show ye,
     Ye'll sweeter sing.

TISANDER   Aye, now begin an' mak' pretence
Wi' witchin' wile, an' gleesome glance,
And then, cast up your influence,
     An' shrewd assistance;
But I hae yet a sort o' sense;
     So keep your distance.

MUSE   Why man, ye sought me mony a time,
To aid you, makin' up a rhyme;
Now, when wi' energy sublime,
      I come, I'm treated
As if some past the common crime
      I had committed.

TISANDER   A crime! a crime! an' did ye not?
Ye did, I'll prove it on the spot:
Ye plainly dealt a partial lot,
      The world may see,
If they but view what *Drummond* got
      Compared wi' me.

MUSE   I think ye needna bounce a bit
For that, but soberly submit,
Ye got your favourite sort o' wit;
      He got nae mair,
But only he was form'd fit
      For twa folks share.

TISANDER   E'en that, shows plainly ye intended
That I should still be less befriended;
Yet like a genius, ye attended
      Baith *Boyd* an' him;
And now, on Fame's wings wide extended,
      See how they swim.

MUSE   Swim! aye, an' may they swim an' shine
An' so they should, an' a' their kin',
How few are form'd to feel sae fine?
      Scarce ane in ten;
Some feel like sheep, an' some like swine;
      But few like men.

TISANDER   So, what I trembl'd at, is true,
That I'm amang the swinish crew,
That what they're bid, dare only do,
      Nor ever tire;
But grumphie-like, maun gruble thro'
      Baith mud an' mire.

MUSE
> Ye needna storm, because ye stan'
> Amang the ignoramus clan;
> As nature taught ye, tell, my man,
> > The thing ye think,
> And I'll be ready at your han'
> > To mak' it clink.

TISANDER
> Ye wadna like to be a dweller,
> Deep in a damp unwholesome cellar,
> An' wi' a stammerin' story teller,
> > That scarcely knows
> The big A's; yet, a rank repeller
> > O' pithless prose.

MUSE
> Na, sic a place as that, I swear
> I hate, an' will for ever mair;
> My pupils in the open air
> > Delight to dwell;
> So, if ye would the laurel wear,
> > Forego the cell.

TISANDER
> Ye ken the wab maun be put out
> To pay the rent - that's past dispute,
> Else Starry, inoffensive brute,
> > Will be tane up;
> Then drammock, dry, (or waur) I doubt,
> > I'd hae to sup.

MUSE
> Ye ken what that is, lang ago,
> Then let it come to pass, or no',
> Here by this brattlin burn, below
> > This bush o' broom,
> We'll pass a pair o' hours, or so,
> > Let what will come.

TISANDER
> I'm wearied, therefore, I agree
> That ye may cheer me up a wee;
> Och! Fortune surely doesna see
> > My constitution,
> Or, some time, she had smil'd on me
> > In retribution.

MUSE

Tho' forc'd to live in vassalage,
Within your little hermitage;
And tho' misfortune, ramp an' rage,
    Ye may defy her;
Ye hae a frien' that can assuage,
    Her fiercest ire.

TISANDER

Aye, if ye wad but cast an e'e
Across that flowery vale, ye'll see
The mansion of the friend, so free
    O' spite an' teen,
That aye the mair ye skaith, he'll be
    The mair your frien'.

MUSE

Then scorn a lowerin' look to wear;
Contemn that peace-destroyer - care,
Above depression's grovlin' glare,
    Arise victorious;
A noble soul delights to dare
    Each thought inglorious.

TO THE PRINCE REGENT

GREAT sir; for everybody owns
They're very great that sit on thrones;
An' rumour commonly agrees,
That they can do what e'er they please;

So ye can spread your royal wing,
As far as ony ither King;
Can stem, at will, the starkest strife,
An' deal about ye, death or life,
As ane wad do a deck o' cards,
Amang baith commoners an' lairds;

Besides, the voice o' fame assures,
That just a single word o' yours,
Can take a booby frae a byre,
An' sen' him forth a gentle 'squire;
An' that wi' you, it's labour light,
Frae naething, to produce a Knight;
Or wi' a sign frae whar ye sit,
Can form a famous Baronet,
Can tak' a common country carl,
An' fashion him into an Earl;
An' what is still a task sublimer,
Can mak' a marquis o' a rhymer,
Or o' a ninny in a neuk,
In twa three minutes mak' a Duke;
In short, ye can do ony thing,
E'en o' a cottier mak' a King.

Now since ye can perform wi' ease,
Sic famous feats whon e'er ye please,
I think, for certain, I'll get soon
My next to naething o' a boon,
Which is to fill yon vacant seat,
That *Bellingham* made i' the state.

As cunning as a *Fox* I'll sit,
An' deep as the profoundest *Pitt.*
I hae a body an' a spirit,
Nor do I mutton hate or claret;
What hinders then my exaltation,
Whon I'm sae fit for 'ministration;
Just wink or nod your royal head,
An' that will quickly do the deed.

I know that seat has mony seekers;
Wha fish for it, by fine fore-speakers;
But I'll tak' nae near cuts about it;
Be thankit - I can live without it:
I'd rather far expire in fetters
Than cringe to you, or e'en your betters;
Yet ye may b'lieve it as your creed,
I fain would *Perceval* succeed,
An' if I do, it's my opinion,
I'll wonners work in your dominion.

Our Marquis in my cause will join,
For he's amaist a frien' o' mine;
The generous Earl will back me too,
An' twa sic charmin' chiels an' you
Whon join'd thegither, quickly can
Mak' o' me just the Gentleman;
That I am almost sure to be,
The instant you this letter see;
But mark my liege, whon you endeavour
To get or keep a great man's favour,
Ye maunna keep him in suspence,
For at this crying-out offence,
He'll cock his nose an' snort an' snuff -
Ye know my meaning - that's enough -
So fare ye weel;- I hope to boast
An answer, by the morrow's post;
But frank it, for I'm scarce o' money.

THE MAKING OF A MAN

THE King on a throne, who can set himself down,
Belov'd by the people of country and town,
May say for a certainty, sure of renown,
    It's monarchy makes the man.

The Statesman will study to settle such laws,
As may from the house, gain the loudest applause,
For then they will tell him in hearty huzzas,
    It's policy makes the man.

The Gallant and Gentleman often combine,
In praise of the comforts of women and wine;
They'll say at assemblies and balls, where they shine,
    It's pleasure that makes the man.

The Minister piously preaches and prays,
And bids us be mindful to mend in our ways;
Then nods with his head, and most solemnly says,
    Religion still makes the man.

The Scholar, who fondly would feast on the foliage,
That springs from the ever-green branches of knowledge,
Cries as he comes home in a fuss from the college,
    It's learning that makes the man.

The Poet sits puzzling all night o'er his pen,
Here scribbling a sentence, there blotting out ten;
And if he succeed, as he seldom does, then
    It's nature that makes the man.

The Quack, if he visit you, talks about nought,
So much as the wonderful cures he has wrought,
He'll bid you of laud'num take daily a draught,
    For medicine makes the man.

The Soldier surrounded by foes in a ring,
Can die like a hero, triumphant, and sing,
O death! what art thou to my country and King?
    It's honour that makes the man.

The Beau struts about every day in his best;
His soul is well pleased, when his body's well dress'd;
He says, when he looks at his fine silken vest,
    It's clothing that makes the man.

The Gamester, who often addresses the ninny,
With - sir, you have spirit, you'll play for a guinea;
Will shout, when he tricks him out of his last penny,
    It's fortune that makes the man.

The Drunkard who all he can scramble up drinks,
And cares not a farthing what swims or what sinks;
In spite of religion and reason, still thinks,
    It's whiskey that makes the man.

The Glutton has ever an appetite, able
To equal the best epicure at the table;
He'll tell you that abstinence is but a fable,
    It's mutton that makes the man.

The Miser, full fifty feet deep in a delf,
Will plunge for a penny to put to his pelf;
Then joyfully count it, and say to himself,
    It's money that makes the man.

Another poor wretch, but I know not his name,
Lives hid in obscurity, shut out from fame,
And thinks that assurance is only a shame
    When modesty makes the man -

The Beggar cries as he comes up to the door,
O, Sir, would you lend a relief to the poor?
Its only but lent, for we're all very sure
    It's charity makes the man.

The Pick-pocket cries, he is rob'd in the fair,
The Cozener - he's cheated will solemnly swear;
And a Thief will be ever the first to declare
    It's honesty makes the man.

But now in conclusion, observe by the way,
If these verses live but a year and a day,
Along with their Author, I'm certain you'll say,
    It's nonsense that makes the man.

ON THE APPOINTMENT OF THE EARL OF MOIRA
TO BE GOVERNOR GENERAL
AND COMMANDER OF THE FORCES IN INDIA

MONARCH of the fearless Britons,
    Bid thy choicest sail prepare
For thy choicest friend's admittance;
    Choicest seamen tend him there.

Steersman! mind thy task intently;
    Bursting billows cease to roar;
Blow propitious gales, blow gently;
    Waft him safe to yonder shore.

O Bengal, rejoice for ever;
    Strew his steps with flowrets fair;
Moira's equal surely never,
    Never breath'd your sultry air.

If your sons be loyal hearted,
    He is noble, gen'rous, kind;
He's the friend that ne'er departed,
    Leaving worth in want behind.

Disappointed sons of Erin!
    Take ye comfort, he's assigned
A more glorious task;- so herein
    Be submissive, be resigned;
He must fill a nobler station,
    He must o'er the Indian deep,
He must bless another nation,
    'Tho' he leave his own to weep.

May all happiness betide him;
    Heaven defend him from his foes!
May his guardian angel guide him
    Safe thro' life, wher'er he goes;

May thy presence round him hover,
    Essence pure of lasting love;
All his brilliant actings over,
    Call him to thy court above.

AN ADVERTISEMENT

ATTEND ye truants, in a trice,
Wha wit sud buy at ony price,
And you, ye learned, great an' wise,
    Ye reverend, holy ban',
O! take a friendly fool's advice,
    An' place nae trust in Man.

And next, ye lusty lasses a',
Ye buxom blossoms, blythe an' braw,
Put ye nae trust in men ava,
    Tho' flatterin'ly they fawn;
But keep them at arms-length, awa',
    For Man is, only Man.

And ye to disappointment's lash,
As senseless as a tinker's ass,
Tho' bless'd beyond the crack-scull class,
    Wi' happiness in han',
Ye seldom lose a thought, I guess,
    On either Gude or Man.

If ye're a Man o' sober sense,
An' wish for to maintain your mense,
Grow great thro' dint o' diligence,
    As quickly as ye can;
Make princes not your confidence;
    It's vain to trust in Man!

If ye're in a contented case,
Ye're happy in whatever place,
Despite his lordship an' his grace,
    For a' sae great an' gran',
If ye enjoy internal peace,
    Ye're blessed, but not by Man.

And you, to your ain lesson lost,
Frae ill to waur, sae prone to post
Ye rhymin' wretches, wretched most
    Of a' the wretched clan;
It's you that ken it to your cost,
      The faithlessness o' Man.

Since ye're sae bent to break the but,
Sae wretched apt to slip the foot,
Keep close within your wattl'd hut,
    There speechless spen' your span,
And O! be warn'd by me, and put
      Nae confidence in Man.

And since, at best, your listless lays
Can scarce procure you paltry praise;
Dear brither-heirs o' blasted bays,
    While on the stage ye stan',
Mind what the Rector's Rhymer says,
      It's vain to trust in Man!

THE DRUNKARD'S FATE, INSCRIBED TO T.T. ESQ.

I own, Sir, it's odd; - it's absurd to request
You to peep at a picture you're known to detest.

DEAR THOMAS, quat your merry springs,
Your fiddle, an' your fiddle strings;
Gie owre a wee your skips an' flings,
    An' tak' a seat,
An' listen while your bardie sings
    The Drunkard's fate:

Behold him! how he lurks an' stays
About the ale-house, half his days,
While oaths and horrid blasphemies
    Employ his breath.
O, shun his works! an' shun his ways,
    As you would death.

See, how he wiles his neighbour in,
Wi' - 'Sir, ye'll tak' a glass o' gin;
Damn hell, it's neither shame nor sin,
    Let wha will know;
Deil hae them drap we'll taste but ane,
    An' then we'll go.'

Then grips him kindly by the han',
An' thus deludes the simple man:
So, in they're gane, an' till't they're fa'n,
    Brisk, baith thegither;
The wretch then whispers, - 'boy its gran',
    We'll hae anither.'

But still the varlet's laith to flit,
So, maun hae mair, an' mair o't yet;
Then cries - (tho' he can scarcely sit),
    'Let him be curs'd,
An' hurled head-long to the pit,
    That rises first.'

'Do we regard the sons of men?
It's honestly our ain we spen';'
Then to the riggin', wi' a sten
    His hat he flings,
An' wi' his social neighbour, then
    Shakes hands, an' sings
'We'll drink till we fall, and we'll pay for it all
And who would not drink good liquor, brave boys.'

Some leuker-on begins a sneerin';
Frae singin', then he fa's a swearin',
And aff his back, in pieces tearin'
    His tattered coat.
An' b'lieve me, Sir, he's hard o' hearin'
    That hears him not.

His neighbour ne'er had seen before,
Nor heard a human devil roar,
So, tremblin' pays the double score
    For peace's sake;
The landlord then, without the door
    Soon lands the rake.

Leuk at him now! see how he goes!
See how his steekit neeve he shows!
Now watch the pavement and his nose
    How fast they'll meet,
An' hear him damn his blood, that flows
    An' stains the street.

Tho' nane molest him, out he calls -
'Foul play, ye dog,' and up he sprawls;
Then twa-three steps before he falls,
    He runs ram-stam,
Then down he goes, and out he bawls
    The tither damn.

He strives to rise, an' then he stumbles,
An' thro' the gutter-hole he rumbles,
Till heels owre head at last he tumbles -
    'You lie,' he cries,
'It's not a roun',' then fykes an' fumbles,
    But canna rise.

So, like a sow, thro' mud an' mire
He wallows, till himsel' he tire,
Then whon he scarcely can respire,
    They drag him out,
And in some dirty roofless byre,
    They throw the brute.

There like a very beast he lies,
From whence he never more shall rise;-
He's dieing now - his reeling eyes
    See how they glare!
He breathes his last, his spirit flies -
    But where? O! where?

Thus, without either rape or knife
He finishes the mortal strife;
The value o' a virtuous life
    Owre late he learns,
So, leaves a broken-hearted wife
    An' beggar'd bairns.

CRIME AND PUNISHMENT
TO THE REVEREND I.P.

DEAR SIR, they say that sic as you,
Can read a tale, if it be true;
    Weel this ye ken yoursel',
That I had never nae desire
To rank me wi' an arrant liar -
    But listen, an' I'll tell:

It was (if I remember right),
Upon a dark December night,
    When hail an' rain severe,
Burst from each blast that Boreas blew,
And fire, in flamin' flashes flew
    Thick thro' the gloomy air.

While deep resoundin' thunders rattle,
Sonorous as the din of battle,
    Where ruin rages round;
This, louder still than that before,
Wild echo, lengthening out the roar,
    Made horror still abound.

Now, terror shook her grizzly plume,
Predicting man's approaching doom,
    An' time's eternal fall.
I thought I heard the trumpet loud,
I thought I saw th'immortal crowd
    "Close clustering at the call."

I thought I saw the heavenly band,
In regular succession stand
    Around the mighty throne,
And vengeance brandishing her sword,
Impatient waiting for the word,
    To sieze upon her own.

While thus imagination wrought
In fancy's field, I heard (me thought),
    Without the door a din;
Wi' tremblin' hand I lift the latch,
When lo! a weather-beaten wretch,
    Half dead, came staggering in.

Wi' care I kittl'd up the coal,
Conscious what houseless wretches thole
    Sic nights, when far frae hame.
And soon as he came to himsel',
I speer'd at him, if he could tell
    His country and his name;

What bus'ness he had been about,
Or what ill win' had drove him out
    In sic wild wasteful weather;
Or why he lodgin' didna get,
When a' the elements were set
    To wrastle wi' each ither.

He sigh'd, but little answer made;
At length, he shook his head, and said,
    Vice has it's ain reward,
And often is repaid in kind,
For harden'd hearts not seldom find
    Hearts equally as hard.

This, sad experience lets me know,
And this, I think, I'll plainly show,
    If ye will lodgin' lend.
I granted that for which he pray'd,
He thank'd me kindly for't, an' said,
    Now to my tale attend:

I once possess'd a fair estate,
And had attendants too, to wait
    Upon me when I pleas'd;
But, wherefore o' my greatness crack,
When underneath a pedlar's pack,
    My back maun now be brees'd.

But how I to sic greatness grew,
Is what I want to show to you,
    That ye may see an' shun;
I had a confidential pair,
That did my business to a hair -
    A servant and a son.

We took a' gaits to gather gear,
My son would lie, my servant swear
    What e'er my son would say;
To ane anither's hands we wrought;
I plotted privately, an' thought
    Soon to be great an' gay.

About the blue time o' the year,
When scarcity the wretched fear,
    An' beggars crowdin' come,
It was my custom every day,
To bid them bolt the gate, an' say
    There's nobody at home.

Thus, what we had, we held secure,
Regardless o' baith rich an' poor,
    Nor thought on heaven or hell,
Till sic a night as this - alake!
When worlds did seem to reel to wreck,
    This incident befell:

A wight bewilder'd, wanders in,
While pendant frae his chitterin' chin,
    Drops, frozen snow-drops hung;
His hoary haffet-locks were a'
Close cloted wi' the drivin' snaw,
    Whar to his cheek they clung.

He sought to lodge till 'twad be day,
As now, he could not find his way
    Thro' darkness so obscure -
Soon was deny'd his humble suit;
My orders were - go, turn him out,
    An' quickly bar the door.

But in the morn, how shock'd was I,
To see the out-cast wanderer lie
 Quite breathless, stiff an' caul';
Close by the porch he lifeless lay!
We knew not what to do or say;
 We were confounded all.

The dropin' eve had washed awa
Frae aff his face the meltin' snaw;
 O, what a sight to see!
His eyes turn'd up, as he departed,
That look - my guilty conscience darted;
 He look'd, I thought, at me.

The news like light'ning flew an' flam'd;
My zealous servant soon was blam'd,
 So was my seckless son;
They had but e'en a ragged name,
False oaths and lies had fil'd their fame;
 So they were seiz'd upon.

A perjured villain, swore aff han',
He saw my servant slay the man;
 So, in a little time
He strangl'd was upon a tree;
A just reward for perjury,
 Which was his greatest crime.

My son was free'd by law, yet still
Was pointed at from every hill;
 The worst may be belied,
As greatest liars often are;
So, being caught in his own snare,
 He broke his heart an' died.

These facts eclips'd my prosperous day;
My wealth took wing an' flew away;
 Thus, fortune whirl'd the wheel,
An' drove me down whar I maun lie
Below her lash, an' feel what I
 Made ithers aften feel;

Which makes me still imagine we
Plain in our punishment may see
    Our most prevailing crime;
Then, let's in time, while time we hae,
In an impartial balance weigh
    Eternity wi' time.

He ceas'd, but left me deep in thought
How worldly things are sometimes bought,
    Dear at the soul's expense;
O! may I ne'er be rich or great,
At so extravagant a rate;
    Better be pinch'd o' pence.

SONNET TO FRIENDSHIP

O, LET me still thy sweets imbibe,
Thou darling of the tuneful tribe!
    Since I have found thee - where?
E'en where the wretched find thee still,
Adorning peace on Parson's Hill;
    Tisander found thee there,
Presiding o'er thy votary's heart
    With absolute controul;
There, plying all thy healing art
    To cheer *Tisander*'s soul.
    So, care then, go where men
    Their span in spite, do spend;
    Here ever, we sever,
    For *T*****'s *Tisander*'s friend.

30th January, 1807.

AN EPISTLE TO BONAPARTE,
ON THE INVASION OF PORTUGAL

O, BONY! BONY! what's this now?
Has hell possess'd your breast? or how?
Or what? or has the de'il and you
    Now faun at odds?
O, scandal! rank affront in view
    O' men and gods.

O, man! I thought you wadna been
In sic a dirty action seen;
I tell you, Sirrah, I'll minteen,
    It files your fame
To rob a broken-hearted queen;
    O, fye for shame!

What way can ye expect success,
Will follow sic an act as this,
To rive an' wreck, an' dispossess
    O' place an' pence,
The widow an' the fatherless,
    For nae offence,

Except it was, for being true
To her best friends, and not to you;
Now, fire an' flint, they'll force 'em through,
    Till they get at ye;
They'll chace ye to destruction's brow,
    Before they'll quat ye.

I'll wad a groat, wha lives to see't,
That Britain's boys will gar ye greet;
For what they gie, they're apt to gie't,
    Sae, without slackings,
That e'en the de'il durst scarcely meet
    Them, without backings.

Sae, up my lad, and dinna jauk,
But quick a moonlight flittin' mak';
And O! take care, for if they track
    Ye on the snaw,
Ye'll never, never mair get back,
     But down ye'll fa'.

But if ye scorn th'advice I gie ye,
I'll no be farther bother'd by ye,
Sae, rin your race, an' de'il gang wi' ye;
    Work on your way;
I dinna care, I never see ye,
     Ye vex me sae.

'Twould vex auld Nick, to see ye commin'
Like some vile vague, in fury foamin',
Against a simple silly woman
    To wreck your rage;
It wad bring credit, Sir, to no man,
     Sic war to wage.

Leuk on, ye man - if *Moira* comes
Wi' a' his fifes, an' a' his drums,
An' a' his bucklers, bayonets, bombs,
    In fury fell;
He'll trample down your lofty plumes,
     As low as hell.

Ye could as muckle bear his bangs,
As *Brueyes* could great *Nelson*'s whangs;
Releasin' lambs frae lions' fangs,
    Was aye his trade;
He still was good at rightin' wrangs
     Whare'er he gaed.

So, keep it secret frae all those
That may the tale to him disclose,
For if ye hae to hear his blows,
    My royal frien',
He'll leave ye wi' a bluidy nose,
     An' twa black ee'n.

Besides, if this disgraceful tale,
Does e'er Sir *Sidney*'s ear assail,
He'll just fa' on ye tooth and nail,
    Full well ye know;
Ye mind he gart ye turn your tail
    No' lang ago.

Sae, hame as hard as ye can lick,
For fear ye get a bain to pick,
Might break your teeth, perhaps, or stick
    Within your gullet;
Ye ken, gin *Geordie* gi'es a kick,
    Ye canna thole it;

An' if you reach your native isle,
Conceal your Bonyship a while,
Till folk forget that deed sae vile
    An' unbecomin',
And never march anither file
    Again' a woman.

24th November, 1807.

TO THE REVEREND T.T. FROM HIS PONY

OCH! och! what's this I'm hearin' noo,
That like a dagger darts me thro',
Or is, or can the news be true,
    That I maun flit?
O Master, Rector, Doctor, do
    Not part me yet;

Keep mind that I was steadfast still,
An' true to you as truth it sel',
I never said or did you ill
    Sin' I was born,
But was obedient to your will
    Baith e'en an' morn.

But since it's sae, that I maun hence,
Sell me to somebody o' sense,
That feelin' haes, an' moderate mence
    Towards beast an' man;
I hope, wi' sic, for sake o' pence
    Ye winna stan'.

'Tis now full fifteen year, at least,
Since I at first becam' your beast,
An' wha I may belang to neist,
    They're wise that know
Be't Duke or Duchess, Pope or Priest,
    I needs must go.

Weel might my master dear, ador'd me,
For wha mair frien'ship could afford me,
Then cheerfully he might restor'd me
    My rack an' sta',
Whon them I never chang'd a word wi',
    Are sorry a'.

E'en there's *Tisander*, whon he'll hear
That ye hae sel't your wee bit meere,
Watch, an' ye'll see the gushing tear
    Start in his e'e,
For, to his heart she was as dear
    As ye're to me.

The Rector may be laith to loss me,
When he laments, that scarcely knows me,
And naething, down-right neathing owes me,
    Plain truth to tell,
Nor ever laid a leg across me,
    Nor ever will.

Poor creature! he was doom'd to paddle
Thro' clabour since he quat the cradle;
He never sat upon a saddle
    O' his ain yet,
Na na, a seat-board or a treadle
    Wad better fit.

Yet still it made me merry-hearted,
When his bit Muse, her skill exerted,
For if only I neigh'd, he gart it
    Turn out a sonnet;
Had I been his, we ne'er had parted
    Till death had done it.

I b'lieve, we scarcely ever yet
Gade by his little garden fit,
But it produc'd upon the bit
    Some rhymin' rant;
Dear save us, but the want o' wit
    's a woefu' want.

Noo, after a' the rattle, I
Your kindness never will deny,
For meat or drink, I would defy
    The worl' to beat ye,
Yet in some measure, by the bye,
    I whiles repaid ye.

Had I like ither brutes been toil'd,
These tidings had na put me doil'd;
Or had I wi' a rung been oil'd,
    When pride was buddin',
But like the fellow's peas, I'm spoil'd
    For want o' roddin'.

I grew as sleekit as a mouse,
Which proves I got na great abuse,
Tho' mony a time I canter'd cruse
    To Mister *M——t*'s,
An' likewise, to the Bishop's house,
    Tho' ten mile aff it's.

We wad a thought it but a sport,
At five, to lea'e Lord *R——n*'s court,
An' hame to Parson's Hill, unhurt,
    By early tea time;
My souple shanks, be thanked for't,
    That fail'd me nae time.

Now, master, let me never sin,
While I'm alive, if I'll gie in
To carry man or mither's sin
    Upon my back,
That wadna care a headless pin
    To break my neck.

So, if ye canna keep me, send me,
An' either sell, bestow, or lend me
To somebody that will attend me
    As weel as *Hammy*,
Len' him his health, he'll recommend me,
    Least ill befa' me.

But best o' frien's maun part - I see,
An' so maun I wi' thine, an' thee,
Therefore, adieu; - my love ye'll gie
    To wee *Mageein,*
For never was there yet to me
    A better bein'.

P.S. They say, a pound o' sorrow yet,
Never has paid an ounce o' debt,
Then henceforth, I will never fret
    What e'er betide:
I'll cock my tail, an' off I'll set.
    The world is wide.

TO W.B. ESQ. THE HUMBLE PETITION OF
HUGH PORTER, OF MONEYSLAN,
MOST HUMBLY SHEWETH,

THAT it petitioner greatly grieves,
That he's perplex'd wi petty thieves,
That this ye needna think a joke,
That they're as plenty as the folk;
That half his pickle peets they tak',
That he has borne upon his back;
That if wi' care, he rear a pullet,
That same maun grease some glutton's gullet;
That if a frien' gies him a hen,
That night her life is at an en'
That e'en his constant-crowin' cock,
That sair'd him nightly for a clock:
That cock they stole - may sorrow switch him,
That had the heart or han' to touch him;
That if his Starry* stolen be,
That he expects to never see
That day he could collect th'gither,
That which would purchase him anither,
That he need never think to waur them,
That has nor sword, nor gun to scar them;
That he had ance a fowlin'-piece,
That lang preserv'd his hens an' geese,
That cost him mair than thirty shillin',
That he gied up in Castlewellan;
That he expected back again
That which was lawfully his ain,
That he sae hop'd - behold the reason,
That he was never blam'd wi' treason;
That if she's gane, and nane kens whar,
That ye will grant him ane nae waur,
That in his morn an' evenin' prayer,
That ye may get a sonsie share -
That ye may aye be rich - but hush,
That is but a superfluous wish;
That ye may still be free o' foes;

That ye may aye hae rowth o' brose;
That far remote the day may stan',
That proves ye but a mortal man;
That mod'rately the stroke may fall
That strikes your body frae your saul.

    That your Petitioner is a wight,
That's nae way tongue-ty'd day or night,
That tells the truth whon he can hit it;
That he's het-headed an' half-witted;
That he's a ram-stam, chace-grace chiel,
That character's him - Sir, fareweel.

Jan. 1808.
* His cow

TO J. J.
A BRITHER RHYMER

HA! Johnny boy, I'll bang ye now,
The laurel's buddin' on my brow;
Na, that's a lie; - I rue, I rue
    That e'er I said it;
'Twas you, stiff-neckit Muse, 'twas you
    To mock me, made it.

There never was a laurel leaf
Ty'd roun' my temple to my grief,
An' to the best o' my belief,
    There never will;
The Muse, confound her dumb an' deaf,
    She gecks me still.

That self-will'd, head-strong giglet, she
Does ought ava she likes for me,
I might as weel attempt to flee,
    As put her fra't,
For when she means to lie, she'd lie
    In spite o' fate.

Since miracles she maun be at,
There let her answer for her faut;
But mony a trick as weel as that,
    She puts upon me:
I'm proud, I'm ought; but liein's what
    I'll never own wi':

It fills me sae wi' spleen an' spite,
That I can neither rhyme nor write;
A something odd, this very night
    I was inventin';
But this has put the hizzie hyte,
    This talk o' printin'.

O printin'! printin'! cream o' craft!
Ye'll sen' me - whar? alaft, alaft;
Ye'll mak' me - what? I marvel aft,
    A - a - a - poet;
O! O! I fear 'twill drive me daft,
    Just thinkin' o' it.

An author! aye, aye, there's the matter
That's better boy, better an' better;-
What am I - no a human creature -
    For see! I'm climbin',
Up - up - I'm up, it's past a clatter,
    And I'm past rhymin'.

Preserve my heart! whar will I light?
Whar will I end my airy flight?
See, see, I'm soarin' out o' sight,
    On Fame's fair feathers.
Fareweel my frien', and O! guid night,
    My glorious blethers;

But haud, I'm comin' to my wit,
I'm getin' better o' the fit;
Th'inchantment's broke, and I can sit,
    An' calm consither
The hale as nonsense, and I'm yet
    Your babblin' brither.

24th Feb. 1808.

ON BEING ASKED WHY POETS ARE POOR
AND SELDOM CONTENTED

ONE reason that poets are poor,
    Misfortunes do often await them;
Another, as solid I'm sure,
    They're simple, and most people cheat them.

And that they are seldom content,
    I think that this plainly determines;
'Twould make a Right Reverend relent,
    To dig in a ditch and make sermons.

Besides, my good Sir, you will find
    This maxim is true, if you study,
The body was made for the mind,
    And not the mind made for the body.

Who ever two masters doth serve,
    The one or the other abuses;
So, they of necessity swerve
    From mammon, or else from the Muses.

While ye sleep on soft beds, unsound,
    They're snorin' on straw - if ye saw them,
While ye have a benefice, bound,
    They scarce have the nails for to claw them.

O! if they could live on the air,
    If nature had cloath'd them in feather,
His Grace the gay garland would wear;
    He would not go with them to gather.

Poor things! they're still treated with scorn,
    And rarely with trust or attention;
I'm alive since before I was born,
    And I never knew one get a pension.

Yet something as wild as the wave,
    Their lunatic brain so bewitches,
That honour, not riches, they crave,
    Yet still they would not despise riches.

Altho' I'm no poet, I wish
    That poets and patrons may never
Abandon their title to bliss,
    But may they enjoy it for ever.

7th March, 1808.

ON THE SUPPOSED LOSS OF A FRIEND

FLOW, ever flow, my gushing tears,
For oh! my too-well founded fears
    Are more than realiz'd!
When will my sick'ning sadness end?
How, how again enjoy the friend?
    The friend so highly priz'd;

In whom the very essence dwelt
    Of purest tenderness,
Who's sympathetic soul could melt
    For e'en a foe's distress;
For him, how I swim now,
    Thro' sorrow's swelling seas;
Still stretching and reaching
    At hope, which ever flees.

30th March, 1808.

A SOLILOQUY
WRITTEN IN A STORM

O! bless me, what an evening's there -
Blast after blast still more severe,
    More shocking still the sound;
The spreading branches from the ash,
Are torn with terrifying crash,
    And tumbl'd to the ground.
I'm weather-beaten with the wind;
    Yea, I'm out-wrestl'd so,
That in me scarcely can I find
    Wherewith to stand or go;

But here's a hawthorn hedge at hand,
In lee of which, a while I'll stand
    And hear the tempest rave,
And view yon heavy-hanging cloud,
As dark as death's heart-shrinking shroud,
    Grim as the gaping grave;
Black emblem of my muddy mind,
    Where once the radiant rays
Of hope, without a shadow shin'd
    In bright unblended blaze.

But now, the haggard eye of care
Pervades my bosom every where,
    And every nook explores
In quest of peace, and if it's found,
It's last remains this hateful hound
    Most dev'lishly devours;
Then raging, rankles in my veins,
    And drinks my bliss away,
And leaves me in the dull demesnes
    Of dark despondency.

Ah, me! my shining summer sun
Of pleasure-yielding youth is gone;
    In infancy, I'm old:
Now health decays, desire dies;
Now fortune frowns, and friendship flies;
    How dim is grown my gold,
Who once could boast so firm a friend?
    As tender and as true
As e'er the sire of souls did send,
    O, toil-worn tribe, to you.

Yet, wherefore, should I mourning go?
I've yet a comforter, and O!
    What better bliss can be,
Than that the powers are pleas'd to spare,
That she that shudders not to share
    A living death with me;
Bereft of this most steadfast stay,
    O, world! what could you give?
What could induce me then a day
    Beneath the moon to live?

But O, Supreme! want what I may,
Grant with this blessing, grant I pray
    Thy glorious gift of grace;
That when I yield my hapless breath,
My safeguard from eternal death,
    May be the Prince of Peace!
For who can wrath inrag'd repel,
    Almighty wrath? or who
With wild devouring fire can dwell,
    And fire eternal too?

Come then, thou infinite I AM,
And with thee, Gilead's blessed balm,
　　To sooth my sin-sick soul;
Come thou, that everlasting art,
And from thine altar, touch my heart
　　With an enkindl'd coal;
Come, in thy gospel's chariot, come,
　　And all my doubts dispel;
Come, rescue me - come, snatch me from
　　The gorgon gripe of hell.

Yes, thou canst conquer all my care,
Canst vanquish dolor, death, despair;
　　Yea, hell itself destroy.
Thou giver great, of greatest things,
Who walk'st upon the tempest's wings,
　　O! grant me to enjoy
Again, the favour of the friend
　　Of friends the very best,
On whom for life I could depend;
　　With whom I could be bless'd.

SONNET TO DEATH

O! TERROR'S monarch! how I fear
To meet thy desolating spear,
　　Thy dire destructive dart!
Not that alone could shock me, O!
Unfitness for the bitter blow,
　　Still rings my heavy heart;
Yet if sweet health be mine no more,
　　Why stand I ling'ring here?
Shiv'ring on dissolution's shore,
　　Still ent'ring, still in fear,
　　Still staying, delaying
　　For that important morn,
　　When I hence shall fly whence
　　I never shall return.

AN ADDRESS TO POVERTY

O! but ye're an unwelcome guest,
As ever creature's cottage grac'd;
My heart-strings ache to see ye plac'd
 In sic a lodgin';
I wad gie a' I'm worth, amaist,
 To see you trudgin';

Nor, is it wi' my will I wait
Till ye think fit to take the gaet;
For little, I wad break your pate,
 Ye rav'nous rook;
O misery! misery! but I hate
 Your ghastly look;

Ye oft bring wi' ye too, a class
That deeper aye make deep distress,
And naething know o' tenderness
 For ane afflicted,
But aften strive to make him less,
 And less respected;

For proof o' this, the ither day
I met his honour on the way,
I bow'd, and beg'd that he would stay
 A moment wi' me,
But a' that I could do or say
 He wadna see me;

Then, presently he was addressed
By just a coof, o' cash possess'd;
And O! what friendship was express'd
 Between the twa,
While I was scorn'd - and you, ye pest,
 I blame for't a'.

Twa tedious twalmonths now hae pass'd
Since ye fell on me furious fast,
And mony a vengefu' scheme ye've cast
    To overcome me;
But now, my boast, my hope, at last
    Ye've wrested from me.

Baith late an' early, day and night,
I've us'd the utmost o' my might
To put your filthy form to flight,
    But oh! alas!
I ne'er can banish from my sight
    That lang thin face.

I'd rather far that ye would slay me,
Than constantly cohabit wi' me;
For at the last ye're sure to lay me
    Sae wretched low,
That I the joy o' gien' frae me,
    Shall never know.

O, dear be wi' the time, whon I
Could a' your ruthless rage defy;
Then, then, I wad hae scorn'd ti' lie
    Beneath your power,
When glowin' friendship flow'd from T****
    Fresh every hour.

An evening then, at P*****'s Hill
Was weekly spent wi' right good will,
Whar I had easy access - still
    My hope's foundation
Was this, and under every ill,
    My consolation.

But now, my friends, the feeling few
Yield my enfeebl'd frame to you;
Now, desperation darts me thro',
    And worse than all,
The generous T**** has left me too,
    To stand or fall.

Yet, wherefore, should a wretch like me
Be aye complainin', while I see
The worthiest o' the world by thee
    Deeply distress'd;
Let beggin' *Homer* witness be
    Whom ye oppress'd

'Gainst *Virgil* too, your rage ran high,
Whom ye compell'd without to lie;
Cervantes too, by want, to die
    In Madrid city;
So *Spenser* perish'd - fy, O fy
    Upon your pity!

Nae heart, but either stane or steel,
Could ever stan' again' you weel,
Your very leuk wad scar the de'il,
    Or *Bonaparte*;
Though i' the actions o' the fiel'
    They're baith expert.

But, to conclude, between us twa,
I wish the de'il, an' you, an' a'
Alang with *Bonaparte*, may fa'
    As far as me,
That ye may never rise ava,
    So let it be.

    9th Sep. 1808.

TO THE REVEREND T.T.
PARSON'S HILL

DEAR RECTOR,

A stranger is comin' to see ye,
A stranger that twonty lang evenings sat wi' ye,
Wha now has lang lang been depriv'd o' that blessin',
The best he could ever yet boast of possessin' -
But, sir, to speak plainly, like ither plain fellows,
Tho' he sud be strung by the neck on a gallows,
He can bide nae langer frae what he's sae bent for,
So, like the bad weather, he's comin' unsent for;
He kens it's a fashion to send for each ither,
An' comin' unsent for, ye know's but anither;
But what can he do, sir, that's sent for to nae place,
It's heartless to bide a' ane's lifetime in ae place,
An' waur for a rhymer, than ony ae creature;
It hurts his guid name, and it alters his nature,
An' mak's him as crabbed as ony crab could be,
An' gars him be a' things but just what he should be;
Now, sir, if your counsel, your beukes, or your letter,
Can mak' a fool-fellow grow wiser or better,
Perhaps in an hour, or may be in less,
Ye'll see at your dwellin', the writer of this.

H. P*****.

TO ONE WHO DEMANDED INTEREST FOR LENDING
FIVE SHILLINGS A FEW DAYS

O MENCELESS miser! greedy grub,
    Aye for advantage gapin',
I b'live sincerely, ye wad rob
    If ye could get escapin'.

Search a' the world, ye wadna fin'
    A worldlin' to exceed ye,
In daily study, how to grin'
    The noses aff the needy.

You honest? na, ye canna be't,
    Ye narrow-hearted wretch ye,
Ye say, ye wadna steal or cheat,
    Yet folk, I b'live, sud watch ye;

An' tho' ye're rich as ony Jew,
    Ye've neither peace nor pleasure,
But when ye're sittin' thoomin' thro'
    Your stockingfu's o' treasure;

Yet wi' this glorious golden gear,
    Your time might not be lastin',
For ye might flit an' lea'e it here,
    Some mornin' fresh an' fastin'.

An' few will fret, whate'er befa' ye,
    I think, because I know some
That wadna sigh, suppose they saw ye
    In *Haran's* brither's bosom.

An' whether gold be there, or gain,
    I vow, I never kent yet;
But this I know, if there be nane,
    Ye'll no be weel contentit.

For O, ye had a strange delight
    In gatherin' gear thegither,
Nor could ye think to part a mite,
    Suppose your very mither

In deep distress, on bended knee,
    Sat pleadin' for a penny;
This answer ye were prone to gie:
    The devil sen' ye money.

Such kindness ye hae aften shown
    To ony that apply'd for't;
But yet your friendship ne'er was known,
    Unless ye were weel pay'd for't.

So at this moment were ye seen
    Expiring in a woodie,
There never yet were mair dry e'en
    About a diein' body.

A chance if there wad be ava,
    A sorry heart behin' ye,
For what the spoon put in, was a'
    That ever was within ye.

11th Jan. 1809.

TO MISS ___ ___

MARIA, fair, as ye grow mair
  An' mair a lovely lassie,
Watch roun' ye weel, for fear the deil
  Sud tempt ye to grow saucy.

For if he get, the least inlet,
  He'll gaur ye think your graces
Nae less, nor waur, but mair an' far
  Aboon the human species;

Then, then I fear, a tumble near -
  But listen to my letter,
That ye may bide, a bit aff pride,
  Ye'll fin' ye'll fare the better:

It happen'd sae, the ither day,
  Beyont my expectation,
That I did dine, wi' them that shine
  Out owre a' the nation.

Nae matter wha, ye ken them a';
  But I got sae conceited,
Sae proud an' vain, I thought again
  I was a-new created.

My only fret, was how to get
  Enow o' folk to know it;
Guid luck had I, that didna try
  Some shameless shift to show it.

I but cam' out, an' blink'd about
  Me, here an' there, an' yon'er,
Aye thinkin' they wad some whar say -
  Your honour, O, your honour!

I thought in plain, that there was nane
  O ony rank or station,
But what sud stan', wi' hat in han',
  In tremblin' consternation.

Had ye but kent, ye wad hae sent
  Or come yoursel' an' watch'd me,
For ne'er a one, I'm sure frae Dan
  To Beersheba, could match'd me.

But hame I go, like ony beau,
  Possess'd o' pride past tholin',
That wadna flinch a fit, an inch
  For *Nickie*, nor *Napoleon*.

It cam' to pass, a little lass
  I met, that didna know me;
She sudden stop'd, an' down she drop'd
  A courtesy unto me.

Hem, hem, quo' I, and inwardly,
  I wish'd the world were near me,
Baith great an' sma, that they might a'
  Be there to see an' hear me.

Upon my heel, about I wheel,
  An' bigger grew, some inches;
My hat sat snug, on my left lug,
  My hauns, upon my hinches.

While govin' thus, the country 'cross,
  I owre a stane fell headlang,
An' there I got a mark, will not
  Be aff me till I'm dead-lang.

Now ye may guess, I'm in distress,
  When my condition such is,
That if I staun, or go, it maun
  Be cripple-like, on crutches.

So here I lie, an' daily cry
  Full mony a loud alas for't;
I rue it sair, for O severe!
  I suffer i' the flesh for't.

I see conceit, however great,
  Will never change our nature,
Nor mak' us mair than what we are,
  Nor better, nor yet greater.

I canna write, nor yet indite
  A bit the mair sublimer,
Which lets me see, I'll never be
  But just the wretched rhymer.

WRITTEN THE NEXT MORNING AFTER HAVING
DINED AND SUPPED WITH THE
REV. MESSRS. T. AND B.

WHAR is the man, that could compute
What e'en ae night can bring about?
Yestreen, on Parson's Hill, my snoot
    I cock'd, like - wha could tell what?
This morn immers'd in smoke an' soot,
    I'm like - I ken mysel', that -

Yestreen, sedate I sat beside
My T****, my frien', my country's pride,
An' him wha cross'd the ocean wide,
    An' brought us owre fu' cantie,
Upon a smooth castalian tide,
    Th' Italic *Homer, Dante.*

Yestreen, like some great knight or squire,
I loll'd upon a cushion'd chair,
An' fed on rich an' dainty fare,
    Whar kindness aye comes gratis;
This morn, I on a stool maun share
    A breakfast o' potatoes.

Yestreen the privilege was mine
To drink the rich an' rosy wine
Like ony favourite o' the nine,
    And what's a serious matter,
This morn, the produce o' the vine
    Is turn'd, wi' me, to water.

Yet, water, for to tell the truth,
Is famous aye for quenchin' drouth;
If we dislike it, in the mouth
    We needna let it dally;
Whon past the pallet, then forsooth,
    It does a body bra'ly;

But on the hale, I've learn'd to know
There's naething certain here below;
E'en *Bonaparte* might be laid low,
    Wha fain our necks wad tread on,
An' whon he gets the hin'most blow,
    Nae matter what he fed on.

TO THE MOST NOBLE
THE MARQUIS OF DOWNSHIRE

MY LORD,

While friends an' folk o' fame,
Wi' compliments salute ye,
    I maun contented sit at hame,
An' barely think about ye.
However ye may end, I'm sure
    Ye make a braw beginnin',
So, may your fame be still as pure
    And clean as new bleach'd linen.
Stan' forth for Erin's honour aye,
    Whar *Downshire's* Marquis should stan'
By birth, if he would live an' die,
    A glorious, great, an' good man;
And still be humble as ye are,
    The nation will adore ye -
Then far and near, e'en every whare,
    Ye'll drive the world before ye:
For them that scarce dare hope to share
    The boon your bounty's bringin',
'Twad glad your Lordship's lugs to hear
    Them at their supper, singin'
'O may our Marquis happy be,
    And healthy, e'en an' morning,
An' live his birth-day feast to see
    Twice fifty times returning;
And when the Powers are pleas'd to flit
    That generous soul they've given,
May he be handed up to sit
    Upon a throne in heaven;'
For me, whate'er I may endure
    O' plentiness or starvin',
Wi' due respect, my Lord, I'm your
    Devoted, humble, servan',

H. P*****.
    8th October, 1809.

ON THE ACCIDENTAL DEATH OF
A FAVOURITE POINTER

YE youthfu' sportsmen, far and near,
Wha like a day's divertion dear,
Approach an' see me sittin' here
    Wi' grief surrounded,
An' drap a sympathetic tear -
    My Grouse is wounded.

Behold in lamentable case,
The best o' a' the settin' race!
Ah me! before my very face
    There pantin', lyin'
In gaspin' anguish - Oh, alas!
    My Grouse is dyin'.

There's mony an ill bred bitches' son,
Thro' pots an' pans, wad sneakin' run,
But he wha's days will soon be done,
    Was better bred;
For now he's goin' - O! he's gone!
    My Grouse is dead!

Now, flow ye briny fountains, flow,
Sad witness of heart-wrecking woe,
Amidst his wanton gambols, lo!
    To ruin hurried;
But hush! let it suffice, to show,
    My Grouse is buried.

THE EPITAPH

Hard by this rock, bedeeked wi' fog,
There lies, a past the common dog,
    For reptiles foul, a feast;
Ye'll soon conclude, he wasna bad,
Whon this was a' the fault he had,
    That he was born a beast.

9th Nov. 1809.

TO T.J.T. ESQ.

DEAR SIR,

I'm just beginnin' to compose
A rhyme or rather, crack-scull prose,
An' that it may expel your woes
    In haste, is his
Desire and earnest wish, that knows
    What sufferin' is.

O! but we are a wretched pair,
As ever grappl'd wi' despair,
Greetin' an' gowlin' late an' ear'
    Wi' pain an' woe;
How ill we're now, how weel we were
    Some time ago!

But since we can do little else,
Wi' mirth we'll try to sooth oursels;
It's better far for monie ills,
    Than burning blisters,
An' safer too, than draps or pills,
    Vomits, or g———s.

'Tis a' the same I plainly see,
To be o' great or low degree,
When ye're as ill, an' waur than me
    Wi' pain offended;
The only odds is, ye can be
    Better attended;

We sudna at affliction spurn,
Nor faint, because we're made to mourn,
But kiss the rod, an' to it turn
    Wi' full intent,
Least wrath, infinite wrath sud burn
    Ere we repent;

But blyther scenes wad better fit
Us baith, at this important bit,
Then let us down thegither sit,
    An' sing, an' laugh,
An' mix a dose o' mirth an' wit,
    An' drink it aff.

Auld Orpheus play'd sic merry strains,
He charm'd the very sticks an' stanes;
Then try to charm your aches an' pains,
    For ye hae skill;
But I can only bother brains,
    Do what I will.

I canna bear to use a treadle,
Nae mair can ye, a chaise or saddle -
Weel, since these pass-times ye were bred till,
    Sma' joys impart;
Back-gammon, maybe, or the fiddle
    Wad cheer your heart.

And I'll prepare me too, wi' speed,
To tune my harp or oaten reed;
An' may the Muse her votary lead
    To sic a lay,
As may intice his T**** to read,
    An' smile, an' say,

'Can my Tisander sing so well,
In poverty's sequester'd cell?
Can he contented daily dwell
    With care and woe,
Or would he only fain excel
    In seemin' so?'

Then tell him, Master Thomas dear,
That acquiescence whiles can cheer
This heart, tho' achin' aft for fear
    O' fell confusion;
But to conclude, at least come near
    To a conclusion. -

If whon I strike the tremblin' string,
But antimelody I bring;
My ill-tun'd harp I'll frae me fling,
    And you alone
Shall play, and I shall after sing,
    By way o' drone.

And may Apollo fan the fire,
Till a' our ailings quite retire;
Then pleas'd, the patron an' the sire
    Shall sit observant,
Which is the hope and sole desire
    Of, sir, your servant.

H. P*****.
 27th June, 1810.

THE LAST SPEECH, AND DYING LAMENTATION OF BALLYWARD LAKE, ADDRESSED TO THE REV. T.T. PARSON'S HILL

O! FRIEND of all that need a friend,
My last lament to you I send,
But mark, it's no your aid I'm wooin',
To snatch me frae impendin' ruin;
Na, na, I know it's lang owre late
For me to think to shun my fate,
But just it does my spirit brace,
To talk wi' ane that kens my case.

Ah! wae is me, the day's at han',
That I maun lea'e my native lan',
To be forgotten quite an' clean,
An' never, never mair be seen;
For Messrs. B— and B— hae said it,
An' wha haes bauldness to forbid it,
And English *John* has mony a slave,
These eight days diggin' at my grave.

Yet still I think, they shudna heed me,
But let me keep what nature gied me;
Yet they're as sick, for that I know,
As *Ahab* was lang time ago,
Whon he lay dying wi' regard
For honest *Naboth*'s boney yard;
So, they by force, before my face,
Will rob, and drive me to disgrace,
An' maybe tear me spaul frae spaul,
Or if they let me live at all,
'Twill be in banishment, forgot
In ditches deep, to lie and rot.

But, sir, as ye shall plainly see,
They sudna first hae fa'en on me,
For aft I've grac'd the board of those
That are my most inveterate foes,

Wha think it neither sin nor shame,
To change my nature an' my name;
But shortly, they'll by force confess,
Th' inferiour qualities o' grass;
Tho' sair'd up in a siller bowl,
O! how unlike my fish an' fowl!
Fowl on my very bosom fed,
And fish within my bowels bred:
The former, nature has supply'd
Wi' wings, that they can flee an' hide;
The latter, harmless, helpless things,
Hae neither legs, nor arms, nor wings,
Nor ought ava for to defend them,
So, ony ane that likes, may end them,
Or frae my tenderness may tear them,
An' quickly to destruction bear them;
But twice twelve hours will end it all,
For Thursday next - ah me! I fall;
The country roun' will a' be here,
At my calamities to sneer:
Such is the fate o' folk in trouble,
They strive to mak' them suffer double.

But yet, the bard beyond the bourn,
I know, at my mishap, will mourn;
For aft he play'd his youthfu' pranks,
An angler on my heathery banks;
But what o' him? he's aye neglected,
An' by the great folk disrespected:
For his epistles, an' petitions,
His eclogues, odes, an' exhibitions,
If they sud fa' before the great,
Wad fare like alm'nacks out of date.
E'en tho' the numbers of his lyre
Were warm'd by pure poetic fire,
They'd prove too chilly to engage
The attention of this luke-warm age;
Yet watch him, for I understan'
He likes to be about your han',
An' so he may - but think on me,

An' think on him - an' when you see
The torrents tumblin' from his eyes,
An' hear him chant my obsequies,
Then join wi' him, for ye can feel
For e'en a foe - but fare ye weel.

19th Sep. 1810.

ON BEING ALONE IN THE REV. T.T.'S PARLOUR
11th October, 1810.

HOW often have I happy been,
    Within these sacred walls!
Where never jaunt nor jest obscene,
    The modest listener galls.

Here volumes, thousands, at my will,
    Diverting lessons lend,
But oh! there's something wanting still -
    The cheerful, generous friend.

How "lingering slow", the minutes pass,
    That fleetly flew before,
And yet the time must be, alas!
    That he'll be here no more:

But hush your gloomy thoughts, be still,
    Such thoughts affection spurns;
I'll hence, and back to Parson's Hill,
    When friendly T**** returns.

TO THE REV. D**** M*****

THOU very reverend, mighty man,
Whilst thou harang'st thy Christian clan,
Or musest on the banks of Ban,
    To pass the time,
Wilt thou at my bit Musie's han'
    Accept a rhyme?

I'm no designin' for to say,
Ye're past the common every way,
That barefac'd wheedlin' wad display,
    Which I detest;
For truth's aye truth, an' flattery
    Is praise misplaced:

Gin fame or learning be a bliss,
Ye've prosper'd baith in that and this,
And as for size an' shapeliness,
    An' finished features,
Ye're just like *Saul*, the son of *Cis*,
    'Mang common creatures.

Ye've *Ajax* strength and *Nestor's* wit,
Ulysses' tongue, whon ye think fit -
Wi' praise undue the ne'er a bit
    I'll e'er bespatter ye,
For *Stentor's* voice is wantin' yet,
    Sure that's nae flattery!

Twad seem to me that ye were made
At first for the heroic trade
Of brandishin' the glitterin' blade
    About your pow,
Whar noddin' plumes an' laurels shade
    The dauntless brow!

I'd like right weel to see you lead
An army, at an army's head
Wi' sword in han', your foamin' steed
    Bitin' the bit;
Just perfectin' some darin' deed
    Unequall'd yet.

O,O, for you an' *Wellington,*
To join, and on *Massena* run,
Fierce as *Achilles* on the son
    Of royal *Priam;*
An' may like fame by you be won
    If e'er you try him!

But tho' I talk of war's alarms,
I hate the shrieks o' slaughtered swarms,
Whar heads an' han's an' legs an' arms
    Are snap'd awa',
Without their leave - but frae sic harms
    Dear save us a'.

O sir, gin fortune wad assign
To me, just e'en a pipe o' wine,
And you to shut your fist on mine
    In frien'ship fast,
I think I wadna much repine
    While it wad last.

But a' that I can say or think
'Bout warlike deeds an' draps o' drink,
Can e'er entice my muse to clink
    Poetic time;
So here I vow I'll spill my ink,
    An' quat my rhyme;

Because in scrapin' up a letter,
I thought she might hae manag'd better,
Yet a' my int'rest canna get her
    To shew her powers;
So since I canna mend the matter
    Farewell, I'm yours.

TO THE REV. T***** M*** R***

THO' whether I'm alive or dead
Is hardly known to Mr. R ——,
Yet aye a weel-wisher he'll fin' me
As lang as there is life within me,
And sure as death my days will end,
I fain would have him for a friend;
No that I'm wantin' muckle frae him,
Nor hae I ought ava to gie him,
Except a rhyme, if he'll hae that
He's get it quickly, ere I quat;
Sae much for preface - now for matter
Wherewith to bungle up a letter,
And here I'm, fykin' in a fisle,
To know whether a pert epistle,
Or sang, or satyre, be the maist
Congenial to his reverend taste.
Some fellows entertain their frien's,
Wi' witches, ghaists, an' fairy queens;
One trav'ler firmly has protested,
He saw a place which ne'er existed;
Anither to our view discloses
The spot whar *Michael* buried *Moses*;
And some their betters to excel,
Describe the size an' shape of *Hell*;
Some talk about ethereal wars,
And some can easy count the stars;
Some say that kingdoms are aboon us,
An' tell us a' that in the Moon is,
An' if they treat Miss Luna fair,
Munchauson kens - for he was there;
Some rhymers raise an unco din,
'Bout consternations they've been in,
Hearin' harangues o' learned rats,
An' manly mice outwittin' cats;
Then whon they labour out their label
They'll own forsooth its all a fable. -
But if ye will attention gie,
Ye'se hear a tale o' truth frae me. -

Twa fellows ance o' equal fame
Did each a place o' profit claim,
They were alike in birth an' breedin,
In leuk alike, alike in cleedin',
The tane was as the tither gude,
And baith were form'd o' flesh and bluid;
In person equally compleat,
They differ'd only in estate,
And in opinion - wha wad get
The place for which they baith were set;
So off they gade wi' nimble pace
To let the Justice ken the case,
Wha had the gi'ein' o' the thing,
A man as great as ony king;
His honour saw at the first sight
They baith had just an equal right,
An' so to end the hale dispute
He bade them lug their purses out;
Wha haes maist cash (quoth he) shall fa'
The place by right, for that's the law;
So when he did the purses view
The tane was toom, the tither fou, -
Then says to him that had the gear,
Ye fairly win, the case is clear,
Ye're fortune's frien' an' shall be mine,
The morrow ye'll come here an' dine;
Then says to him that was rejected,
Sic things ye sudna hae expected,
Gang hame, my frien', an' be at rest,
Folk us'd wi' want can bear it best. -

Now sir, this tale that I hae ended
Is but by verity commended,
Sae if ye dinna like sic bletherin',
Ye'se no be bother'd wi' anither ane,
Yet frae it ony common creature
May see the qualifying nature,
And the prevailin' power o' pelf:
But I beg leave to write myself

Your very humble servant.
H. P*****.

ANSWER TO BURNS' "LOVELY JEAN."

MY *Burns* is gane, I'm left alane,
    My dearest spouse no more
Shall bless my arms, an' praise my charms,
    An' tell them o'er an' o'er. -
We baith confess'd we baith were bless'd,
    But O! transportin' scene,
Too soon ye fled, my *Burns* is dead,
    And I'm no more his Jean!

In summer days whon owre the braes,
    The gentle breezes blaw,
The fields wad ring to hear him sing
    "My Jenny dings them a'";
Nae lover's lass that ever was,
    Nor the most happy Queen
That e'er sat on a royal throne,
    Was half sae bless'd as Jean.

How often he wi' sang an' glee,
    Has charm'd my ravish'd ear,
An' made to glow, this cheek that now
    Sustains the gushin' tear;
Whon by my side my *Burns*, my pride,
    Wad sit him down at e'en,
Few, few could vie wi' me, for I
    Was then his happy Jean.

Nae man alive need ever strive
    To gild my bosom's gloom,
No, no, I swear he breathes not air
    Shall fill my *Robin*'s room,
Wha's pen could paint each lovely tint
    That decks the flowery green,
Wha's haun could twine the laurel fine,
    An' dress it on his Jean.

What raptures thro' my bosom flew
    The day he first was mine,
What joys possess'd this pantin' breast,
    Now left by him behin':
But why complain, departed swain,
    A few short months between,
An' then I come to share thy tomb
    An' be again thy Jean.

REFLECTIONS OCCASIONED BY THE ILLNESS OF
THE REV. T***** T****.

MUSE awake - a scene distressing
    Claims a melancholy strain,
All that made my life a blessing
    Lies upon a bed of pain.

Weary watching, never sleeping,
    Doctor's efforts fruitless all,
Nothing but the voice of weeping
    Murmurs thro' the lonely hall.

Weeping sons - the father ever
    Marks you with his last regard,
Weep you may - your loss can never,
    Never, never be repair'd.

O! ye poor that need protection,
    Let your sighs to Heaven ascend,
Mourn ye sons of sad affliction,
    Mourn for your afflicted friend:

Mourn with lamentation double,
    Thou who dost already bow
Underneath a load of trouble,
    Who will share thy sorrows now?

Who will ever soothe thy sadness,
    Who will smother all thy smart?
Who will gild thy gloom with gladness,
    Who will bind thy broken heart?

None thy lyre will ever listen,
    None will cheer thy spirit - no -
None with generous wine will hasten
    To alleviate thy woe. -

Woful now be thy existence,
    Dormant be thy rhyming skill,
Thou shalt only at a distance
    View the groves of Parson's Hill.

O how fleeting, how beguiling
    Sweetest scenes of pleasure are!
Now there's none to meet thee smiling,
    None to bid thee welcome there. -

But to Heaven's will refer him -
    Mercy pities - mercy spares -
O indulgent Maker spare him,
    Answer thus a thousand prayers.

Ye who watch the walls of Zion
    Pressing forward for the prize,
Ere a bed of death ye lie on
    Live like him "and claim the skies."

12th January, 1811.

ON HIS RECOVERY

HUSH ye sounds of lamentation!
　　Social joys again return,
Bringing cordial consolation
　　To this heart so prone to mourn. -

Discontent now fly for ever,
　　Every trifling care I'll spurn,
Having health and him, I'll never
　　Be again dispos'd to mourn. -

Lately I my sorrow vented,
　　Whilst my bleeding heart was torn,
Now I'm happy - quite contented,
　　Not inclin'd at all to mourn. -

Now again he sooths my sorrow
　　With his wonted tender turn,
'Come *Tisander* - come to-morrow,
　　Come to me - but not to mourn.'

Now the fear of dire disaster
　　I can conquer - I can scorn,
Now I share the rich repast, where
　　None had ever cause to mourn. -

May the smiles of bounteous Heaven
　　Every deed of his adorn!
And may many days be given,
　　For to comfort those that mourn!

Now may anguish never grieve him,
　　May he never be folorn
Till the gates of bliss receive him,
　　Never never more to mourn.

28th February, 1811.

TO THE PRESIDENT AND OTHER MEMBERS
OF THE RATHFRILAND BOOK SOCIETY

DEAR WORTHY SIRS,
                Will ye attend,
Or as I should say, condescend,
      To hear my supplication?
Ye're wi' the truly noble class'd,
And that's the basis where I rest
      My hope and expectation. -

O, if I some great something were,
An' had as muckle cash to spare,
      As might mak' me a member,
And ye wad sic a wretch admit,
Ye'd see how saucily I'd sit
      Amang ye 'ere December.

But miracles are ceas'd, an' so
I sud contented lie below
      My cross - without distraction,
Yet such, alas! my passions are
That I as much could tame a bear,
      As keep them in subjection.

'Tis not for want o' pence, I pine,
Nor want o' pratoes, when I dine -
      Worse, far far worse, assails me,
Aye worse, in almost every sense;
But least I keep ye in suspense,
      'Tis love, 'tis love that ails me:

A Highland lassie, buskit braw,
Wha's face, I'm sure, I never saw,
      Tho' very fair her fame is;
O, how I languish for her sake!
The lovely *Lady of the Lake,*
      For that I think her name is.

She lodges, I'm inform'd, wi' you;
So what ye bid, I deem she'll do
    Without all hesitation.
O, do not then my suit deny,
That on her matchless beauties, I
    My gaze wi' admiration.

Her sire, his approbation gies,
An' so will she, I'm sure, for she's
    A courteous, kindly creature,
An' fitted out in every case,
To gratify the human race,
    For graces and good nature.

I winna, sirs, upon my honour,
Lea'e an offensive haun' upon her,
    Nor nane that would, shall see her;
Na, na, I'd think nae sin to tak'
The rascal's life that would e'en mak'
    The sma'est freedom wi' her.

Indeed she sometimes, may be, may
See twa true comrades that I hae,
    A preacher*, and a plew-man+;
But they're a chaste an' modest pair,
An' few as famous ever were,
    For keekin' clearly through man.

She therefore canna be beguil'd,
Nor frae your humble servant wil'd
    By man, or maid's invention,
For come o' me, or mine, what will,
While she bides wi' me, she shall still
    Command my whole attention.

Now, a' that I desire or seek,
Is just her company a week,
    To keep my spirits cheery;
'Twad mak' me happy, I declare,
To corlie wi' a lady fair,
    At e'en whon I am weary.

Perhaps, 'tis this much labour lost,
For oh! I ken it to my cost,
    I never can command her;
So, I'll put up my quill an' quat,
Tell her I'm truly hers, an' that
    Her lover is
                            TISANDER

26th Sep. 1811.
    * Young
    + Burns

ANSWER FROM THE SOCIETY TO TISANDER

THE *Lady of the Lake*, to you
Returns her thanks and service due;
Nor, tho' the bard of Selkirk sung,
In sweeter notes than ever rung
Thro' Scotia's vales, her deathless praise -
Does she disdain *Tisander's* lays.
'Tis true, she long has left the court
Of Kings and Thanes, the proud resort;
And cannot plead your humble claims
In *Stirling's* hall, to royal *James* -
True, she has left her favourite island,
And now salutes you from Rathfriland:
There she on lofty shelf reclines,
'Mongst sages, poets, and divines;
And hither, in their name invites
Tisander to the pure delights,
That virtue, wit, and solid sense,
By type and paper can dispense:
There you, with all a poet's wonder,
Upon their various lore may ponder,
And rise, perhaps, to loftier lays,
That late posterity may praise,
(If you can gain the nine braw lasses,
That rent out acres on Parnassus,
In fair fee simple, to assign
A rood or twa without a fine),
Then welcome to the bright *Divan*,
Thrice welcome, bard of Moneyslan!

TO MR. G.A.
WHO PROPOSED HIM AS AN HONORARY MEMBER.
1st October, 1811.

PLAIN, honest, downright, *Gilbert Adams*,
(For I'm ill vers'd in sirs an' madams),
I hum ye owre my hearty thanks,
While here I rest my weary shanks,
Within the peet-neuk on a stool,
'Forfoughten sair, wi' spade an' shool,
Which aft hae blistered baith my hauns;
Yet while this fleshly fabric stauns,
An' while fair Phoebus burns aboon me,
I'll min' the honour ye hae doon me.'

Wow! man, but ye hae made me happy;
A bottle o' the stoutest nappy,
That ever yet could boast the birth
O' either anger, wit, or mirth,
Couldna hae made me half sae vauntie,
Or made me 'cock my crest' sae cantie.

The love-lorn wretch, wha lang had born
His sweet-heart's insolence an' scorn,
Resolv'd to terminate the strife,
By snigin' thro' the thread o' life,
To let the crimson current spout,
An' carry the infection out,
For which dire purpose he doth staun,
Wi' grewsome-gully in his haun,
Ready to cut his throat - dear bless us!
Whon lo! the object o' his wishes,
Comes flyin' wi' her heavenly charms,
An' clasps him in her yieldin' arms,
An' bids him hope, an' have, an' live,
And all that honour can, she'll give:
E'en he amid this gush of treasure,
Could not be mair o'er power'd wi' pleasure,
Than I was, when your lady fair,

In answer to my ardent prayer,
Did send and say '*Tisander*, come,
Conduct me to your little home;
Behold, I'm yours by fate's decree,
Deliver'd, sign'd, and seal'd my me,'
     The *Lady of the Lake.*

Now, *Gilbert*, I've nae mair to say,
I'll see you on my nuptial day,
Which ye'll observe is firmly fix'd,
To be sometime December next;
I canna tell the day exac',
For I hae ne'er an almanac;
I'll be beside your frien', the Rector,
My patron, pride, an' benefactor.

   For Master *Sam,** my ither frien',
Pray tell him, *Gillie*, that I mean
To drink his health in water clear,
For that's the plentiest potion here;
But whon to Parson's Hill I fare,
To mak' my weekly visit there,
I'll toast it round in stuff as stout
As ever gade in glass about;
He may depend on that for ae thing,
For I get plenty there for naething,
An' that's the cheapest way o' drinkin';
We'll no dispute on this I am thinkin'.

Tell Rev. B***, the bard of Hillton,
That he's the person I hae built on,
To solemnize my marriage rites,
An' licence me for love's delights.

An' tell the rest that I'll remember
The hin'most Friday o' September;
While I a couplet can contrive,
An' that I hae a heart alive
To frien'ship, tho' I canna show it;
But that's the fate o' mony a poet.
I'd fain string up their names in rhyme,
But want o' paper an' o' time,
Gaurs me abruptly quat my theme -
I've scarcely room to write my name.

TISANDER.

* Samuel Murphy, jun. who seconded, etc.

TO THE MEMORY OF THE LATE
RIGHT REVEREND THOMAS,
LORD BISHOP OF DROMORE

O *Percy*, may the meanest Muse
    That ever tun'd the lyre,
Attempt the dirge, when fatal news
    Sets every soul on fire!

Apollo, do thou teach me skill,
    To swell the solemn sound;
My best friend weeps! can I be still?
    Ah no! let tears abound.

Now *Robinson*, thy Muse alarm'd,
    Shall sound from shore to shore:
Him whom thy infant numbers charm'd -
    Thy *Percy*, is no more!

Ye bards of loftiest note and name,
    Your efforts join in one,
And vent your sadness on your theme -
    Your friend, your patron's gone.

Ye sons of Levi, join the choir,
    The general sorrow share;
And every bough about Dromore,
    The sable cyprus wear.

O *Campbell*, be not silent now!
    Let all thy powers appear;
O *Drummond, Drummond*, where art thou!
    When anguish calls thee here?

Attend ye worthies - do, ah! do
    Produce the funeral song;
I'll chant my little requiem too -
    But far behind the throng:

Yes, far - alas! far, far behind
    The wailing crowd I'll crawl,
And bid ambitious worldlings mind,
    That great men weep, when good men fall!

3rd October, 1811.

THE PROFLIGATE TO ITS AIN TUNE.

I AM a brave jolly brisk boy,
    I daily carouse to keep care away;
A bottle's my life and my joy,
    And makes a dull moment soon wear away;
Let afterwards do as it may,
    I like to have happiness still in han',
If creditors crave me, I'll say,
      'Tis hard to get breeks aff a Highlan'man.

I aft gave the shirt aff my back,
    The full-flowing bumper to bring again;
Then come on the table a crack,
    Till glass and jug I make ring again;
The landlord then calls for his jink,
    I answer, I have not a shillin' man;
And this often pays a good drink,
      'Tis hard to get breeks aff a Highlan'man.

The miser, a purse full of pelf,
    (Perhaps for a spend-thrift), keeps craftily,
But I only care for myself,
    And let him take chance that comes after me;
If any to gambling incline,
    There never was yet a more willin' man;
But soon my gay game-fellows find,
      'Tis hard to get breeks aff a Highlan'man.

Thus, time I pass jovially by;
    And mean, while I live, to live merrily;
What tho' I insolvent should die,
    The priest or the parish will bury me.
My friends do me daily advise,
    But they might as well take the deil in hand;
I want will and power to be wise;
      'Tis hard to get breeks aff a Highlan'man.

TO HIS GRACE THE DUKE OF ——

MAY IT PLEASE YOUR GRACE,

ITS settled on for certain here,
Ye've got sae mickle gowden gear,
    Ye know na how to use it;
In consequence o' sic a talk,
I hae a wee request to mak';
    I think ye'll no refuse it:

I know your Grace can easy grant,
The little yearly thing I want -
    Five hun'er poun's the hale o't;
A very triflin' sum, it's true,
But comin' frae the like o' you,
    A body thinks a deal o't.

Now, whon I hae obtain'd this boon,
(And that, I'm certain, will be soon),
    The people will halloo it,
In every public place, I wean;
'Ho! heard ye that his Grace has gi'en
    A pension to a poet.'

Ha, ha, but I'll be unco cheerie,
Whon hunners, hunners by the year, aye
    Come cannilie unto me.
Whar will I ride, whar will I rin,
This world's owre wee to spen' it in;
    O sirs, what will come o' me.

O for a pocketfu' o' purses!
A coach an' fifty pair o' horses
    To whip me owre to Lon'on!
Whar I'll grow some uncommon thing;
Dear keep me - it might be a king,
    And then I'll sit my throne on.

O bless me, boys, how big I'll be -
I think, I really think I see
    Mysel' subduin' *Bony*;
But haud a wee - I ought to wait,
And no to grow sae glorious great,
    Until I get the money.

EPIGRAM TO A LIAR

O MAN, but ye think much o' truth;
    Ye surely hae a hoard o't
Laid up in store - for frae your youth,
    Ye seldom spent a word o't.
But falsity, ye mak' a slave,
    For every day ye wear it,
While truth, ye like your siller save,
    Aye speakin' lies, to spare it.

AN EPITAPH ON A MISER

HE's flitted, an' whether for waur or for better,
We canna weel say, nor it's no muckle matter;
But this we can safely assert, without study,
A narrower saul never fled frae a body.

ANOTHER

HIS body's buried here,
    And how his spirit fares,
I canna say - but this I'll swear:
    There's nane that kent him, cares.

ON A SPENDTHRIFT

BELOW this bit slate
    He lies lifeless and caul,
That drank an estate,
    An' was dry after all.

ON A SLUGGARD

HE's dead, an' he's rotten, and few for him weepin';
    He couldna be bother'd wi' breath:
He was so extremely delighted wi' sleepin',
    He's lien down to doze here wi' death.

TO A FRIEND IN TROUBLE

O THOU! who's word, whose healing word,
    Has often conquer'd care
Within this breast, and joy restor'd,
    When grief had fester'd there.

O that I in return, could yield
    The blissful balm to thee,
And guide thee thro' the mazy field
    Of grief, as thou didst me.

Thou first and best of friends! O say,
    What theme could heal thy heart?
Tell me - O tell me, that I may
    Pluck thence the deadly dart?

I fain would sympathy avow -
    Fain, fain with thee condole;
I fain would yield thee comfort now
    When anguish wrings thy soul.

O for an angel's tongue, to cheer
    Thy melancholy mind;
But ah! what friendly power will hear?
    What subject shall I find?

A comfort sure it needs must be,
    Amidst a father's fears,
Never to hear the sighs nor see
    The tender mother's tears:

It's true, when health is scarce mature,
    And feeble is the frame,
A wounded spirit to endure,
    Is trouble in extreme;

Yet, on affliction's dreary bed,
    I saw thee not repine;
Tho' hopes of life were almost fled,
    Heav'n's will was ever thine.

Now value health, thy tears forego,
    Let cheerfulness return -
I ask it with a sigh - for O!
    I cannot see thee mourn.

Dec. 1811.

ERIN'S WELCOME TO THE EARL OF MOIRA, ON A REPORT OF HIS BEING APPOINTED LORD LIEUTENANT

YOUR welcome, my *Moira*, the chief o' my kin,
As dear to my breast, as the heart that's within,
Wi' Loudon's fair lassie, the pride o' the plain,
Ye're welcome to Erin, my laddie, again.

Ye left me, my *Moira*, to stan' or to fa',
Wi' nane to defend me frae villains ava;
But now, if they meddle, they'll fin' they're mista'en,
Since *Moira's* come back to auld Erin again.

I own, I provok'd you, my *Moira*, to go,
Yet blood is aye warmer than water, you know;
My Paddies to meet you, will march in a train,
And welcome you back to auld Erin again.

Now rule me, my *Moira*, your will mak' a law;
I'll sleep at your biddin', I'll rise at your ca',
I'll tell my foes roundly, that *Moira's* my ain,
And welcome you back to auld Erin again.

For glory, my *Moira*, ye wander'd right wide,
An' Loudon's fair lassie, to win for your bride;
Now baith ye hae gotten, to pay for your pain,
And mak' ye thrice welcome to Erin again.

Frae Britain, her *Hastings* the laurel may claim;
Her hero abroad, her defender at hame;
A match for my *Moira* she never nurs'd nane,
Then welcome my laddie to Erin again.

TO THE REVEREND T.T. PARSON'S HILL.
ON THE BEGINNING OF THE YEAR 1812.

MY lov'd, my honour'd Patron, say
    Wilt thou again give ear?
Wilt thou again indulge the lay,
    To hail the youthful year.

Twelve times twelve months have roll'd around,
    Since first my simple song
Sought patronage in thee, and found
    The friend I look'd for long.

The first seven years of which I spent
    Without a careful thought;
Then three, on hopes and fears intent,
    And two, with anguish fraught.

But have I anguish felt alone?
    Are great minds free? ah! no,
For my *Macenas* too has known
    Full well the weight of wo.

A little sorrow more, and shut
    Will be the scene of strife;
Fate soon the silver cord can cut,
    That whirls the wheel of life.

'Tis heaven that has that crisis fix'd;
    What angel's arm can save?
This moment's ours - but where's the next -
    Perhaps beyond the grave.

How bless'd the hour that sets us free,
    From such a life, as meets
By Fate's unchangeable decree
    More bitters far than sweets.

Of those few joys this earth can bring,
    My portion is but small:
'Bove nothing - scarcely any thing -
    Existence almost all.

But yet I do not, will not mourn
    Tho' heaven has health deny'd;
The little sordid soul I scorn,
    That would make gain its guide.

Tho' with each hour's returning wheel,
    Returning wants do ask
Exertions great, and tho' I feel
    Unequal to the task,

Yet strange! I almost am content
    When I recount, with glee,
The many blissful hours I've spent
    On Parson's Hill, with thee.

Thy friendship, try'd by time so long,
    Brings honour to my side -
'Tis not myself, 'tis not my song -
    My patron is my pride.

How few of elevated rank,
    But would, with scorn, regard
Th' illiterate, incoherent clank
    Of an ignoble bard?

But thou hast often taught this heart
    To wander from its wo;
Yea often, often smooth'd the smart
    Of many a throb and throe.

Therefore, on prospects fair I gaze,
    And hope anon to see
Far better times, far happier days:
    Amen - so let it be.

TO WALTER SCOTT, ESQ.
ON A REPORT THAT HE WAS TO RECEIVE £3000 FOR
THE COPY OF "ROKEBY."

THREE thousand in a lump - ha, ha;
That wins frae ought I ever saw,
Forby the honour it will draw
    Frae every art to thee, *Wattie*;
Right far the trumpet voice o' fame,
Extends thy glory an' thy name;
But oh! it plays the very shame,
      On little bards like me, laddie.

Each bardie now, tho' ne'er sae keen,
May quat the scribblin' trade, I ween,
For a' the world, wi' earnest een,
    Are glowerin' up at thee, *Wattie*;
Nae poem, now, is worth a groat,
Unless it comes frae *Walter Scott*;
A' rhymers else are now forgot,
      Forgot alang wi' me, laddie.

Full sweetly thou hast Marmion sung,
But sweeter far Lough Cathrine rung;
Now Rokeby sets baith auld and young
    A doatin' about thee, *Wattie*;
O for the gleanings o' thy praise,
To cheer my melancholy days!
But oh! these life-inspiring rays,
    Will never blink on me, laddie.

Yet b'lieve this simple truth frae me:
Tho' I should beg 'em on my knee,
I would five golden guineas gie,
    For leave to leuk at thee, *Wattie*;
The laurel's gatherin' every where,
For Selkirk's honour'd bard to wear;
But oh! there's no' a sprig to spare,
    No, not a leaf for me, laddie.

Bays lately bloom'd on *Burns*'s brow,
Incircling his immortal pow;
But now the garlands only grow
    For *Campbell* an' for thee, *Wattie*,
Thy skill in legendary lore,
Has set thee, ilka bard, before;
To be the king o' a' the choir,
    Thou'lt get a vote frae me, laddie.

TO THE REVEREND T.T.
ON THE DEATH OF HIS ELDEST SON, LIEUTENANT
IN THE 27th REGIMENT, IN SICILY, APRIL, 1812.

A DEEP "indebted Muse," O, T****!
    Would very humbly join
Thy bitter wailings with a sigh -
    Would mix a tear with thine;
Assur'd that thou wilt not repine,
    Nor deeply be concern'd;
That heavenly lesson, to resign,
    Already thou hast learn'd;

'Tis thine to heal the wounds of woe,
    That make the wretched mourn;
'Tis thine to feel the friendly glow,
    That bids the bosom burn;
And oh! 'tis thine to be folorn,
    Which deeper drives the dart;
For fate a tender tie has torn,
    That closely clasp'd thine heart;

I know a very pond'rous part
    Of sorrow is thy share;
I know the throbbings of thy heart,
    When grief inhabits there:
Alas! that ever past'ral care,
    Or sweet paternal peace
Should usher in a pang severe -
    A youthful son's decease!

Upon a foreign shore, alas!
    'Mid strangers to expire!
'Mid soldiers, soldiers pityless,
    Made death itself more dire;
No friend to mitigate the fire
    Of dissolution's dread;
Far from a kind indulgent sire,
    Life's trembling taper fled!

Thy bard presumes not to forbid
    Thy bursting tears to flow;
He knows thy grief cannot be hid,
    So deep thou wad'st in woe;
Yet suffer not that grief to grow,
    Nor fortitude to fail;
Heaven blesses those that bless the blow;
    "Heaven often wounds to heal."

A CONCLUDING ADDRESS TO THE READER.

NOW reader, I'm supposin' you
Hae read this bunch o' blethers thro',
And that ye're wond'rin' what he's like,
That's keepin' sic an unco fyke,
About his ill-digested jargon,
For which ye made sae blin' a bargain.

Come then, observe, he is a callan
That's aye a foe to strife an' brawlin',
Likes peace an' frien'ship won'er weel,
And hates nae creature but the deil;
Ambitious o' a fair-won fame,
An' gets, I b'lieve, an honest name.

(Honest, ye'll say, he canna be,
The scoundrel, for he cheated me;
O! but I was a silly gowk,
To buy a pig within a poke;
But for the time to come, I'll watch him,
And if we meet, I'll may-be match him;
However, as I dinna know him,
Gang on wi' your description o' him);
I winna put his faults in rhyme,
For that would waste owre muckle time,
Besides, if I conjecture right,
He'd rather keep them out o' sight:
Tho' guidness he has little skill o',
He hates to hear guid folk spoke ill o';
And tho' he can baith eat an' drink,
He's no an epicure I think;
O' frien's he has a glorious raw,
Right saucy too he's o' them a',
Yet backward aye amang his betters,
Because he's no a man o' letters;
For learning, there was ne'er a clown,
Knew less about a verb or noun;
Then marvel not suppose he stammer,
That never even read a grammar.

He's nae-way stupid, dull, or sour,
But whon folk would him paddle owre;
That he could never weel abide,
His passions were sae ill to guide;
In spite o' reason, care, or craft,
A disappointment drives him daft.

These hints, his inward powers comprise;
Now for his outward shape an' size:
He's midlin' feat, an' pretty straight,
Just ten stane, even-beam, in weight,
In height, exactly five feet seven;
His age twice five an' twice eleven;
No clumsy made nor nicely bred,
Nor brag'd o' or for white or red;
His hair a sort o' sooty pale,
An' tho' his pelt be brown, it's hale;
He's neither strong nor very healthy,
Nor just a beggar, nor yet wealthy;
His daily pratoes he gets fairly,
By workin' ident late an' early;
And if description true be given,
He's neither fit for earth nor heaven,
Nor life, nor death, nor ought I ken o';
But this address to mak' an en' o',
In Moneyslan his little hame is,
A wattl'd cottage - an' his name is

HUGH PORTER.

EXTRACT FROM 'THE IRISH CABIN'
BY PATRICK BRONTË

A light its pale ray faintly shot,
 (The snow-flakes its splendour had shorn,)
It came from a neighbouring cot,
 Some called it the Cabin of Mourne:
A neat Irish Cabin, snow proof,
 Well thatched, had a good earthen floor,
One chimney in midst of the roof,
 One window, and one latched door.

Escaped from the pitiless storm,
 I entered the humble retreat;
Compact was the building, and warm,
 Its furniture simple, and neat.
And, now, gentle reader, approve
 The ardour that glowed in each breast,
As kindly our cottagers strove
 To cherish, and welcome their guest.

The dame, nimbly rose from her wheel,
 And brushed off the powdery snow,
Her daughter, forsaking the reel,
 Ran briskly, the cinders to blow:
The children who sat on the hearth,
 Leaped up, without murmur or frown,
An oaken stool quickly brought forth,
 And smilingly bade me sit down.

Whilst grateful sensations of joy,
 O'er all my fond bosom was poured,
Resumed was each former employ,
 And gay thrifty order restored:
The blaze bickered up to the crook,
 The reel clicked again by the door,
The dame turned her wheel in the nook,
 And frisked the sweet babes round the floor.

Released from the toils of the barn,
　　His thrifty blithe wife, hailed the sire,
And hanging his flail by her yarn,
　　He drew up his stool to the fire;
Then smoothing his brow with his hand,
　　As, if he would sweep away sorrow,
He says, "Let us keep God's command,
　　"And never take thought for the morrow." ...

But later, and later its wearing,
　　And supper they cheerfully bring,
The mealy potato, and herring,
　　And water just fresh from the spring.
They press, and they smile: we sit down;
　　First praying the Father of Love,
Our table with blessings to crown,
　　And feed us with bread from above. ...

EXTRACT FROM 'EPISTLE TO
THE REV J— B—' BY PATRICK BRONTË

When warm'd with zeal, my rustic muse,
Feels fluttering-fain, to tell her news,
And paint her simple, lowly views,
    With all her art,
And, though, in genius but obtuse,
    May touch the heart.

Of palaces, and courts of kings,
She thinks but little, never sings,
But wildly strikes her uncouth strings
    In some poor cot,
Spreads o'er the poor her fostering wings,
    And sooth's their lot.

Well pleased is she, to see them smile,
And uses every honest wile,
To mend their hearts, their cares beguile,
    With rhyming story:
And lead them to their God, the while,
    And endless glory. -

Perchance, my poor neglected muse,
Unfit to harass, or amuse,
Escaping praise, and loud abuse,
    Unheard, unknown,
May feed the moths, and wasting dews
    As some have done.

Her aims are good, howe'er they end -
Here, comes a foe, and there, a friend,
These point the dart, and those defend,
    Whilst, some deride her;
But, God, will sweetest comforts blend,
    Whate'er betide her.

Thus, heaven-supported, forth she goes,
Midst flatterers, critics, friends, and foes;
Secure, since He who all things knows,
    Approves her aim,
And kindly fans, or fostering blows
    Her sinking flame.

Hence, when she shews her honest face
And tells her tale, with awkward grace,
Importunate to gain a place
    Amongst your friends;
To ruthless critics leave her case,
    And hail her ends. ...

GLOSSARY

A

A,	all
Aboon,	above
Ae,	one
Aff,	off
Aiblins,	perhaps
Ain,	own
Alang,	along
Amang,	among
Amaist,	almost
An,	and
Ance,	once
Ane,	one, pron. "yin"
Aneath,	beneath
Anent,	against
Anither,	another
Auld,	old
Ava,	at all
Awa,	away

B

Ba,	ball, the earth
Bairns,	children
Baith,	both
Ban,	to swear
Banes,	bones
Bauld,	bold
Beet,	fewel added to fire
Befa',	befal
Beuk,	book
Biggin,	building
Bit,	nick of time, crisis
Blaw,	blow
Blether,	idle talk
To blink,	to shine by fits
Bluid,	blood

Bony,	pretty
Braes,	declivity, slope of a hill
Braw,	handsome, fine, brave
Brattling,	hurrying
Brees,	bruise
Brithers,	brothers
Brose,	porridge
Bun,	bound
Burn,	water, rivulet
Buskit,	dressed
Byre,	cow stable

C

Ca,	call
Callan,	boy
Cam,	came
Camp,	to struggle for superiority
Canna,	cannot
Cannie	gentle, dextrous
Cantie,	merry
Carle,	old man
Cauldrife,	chilly or cold
Chiel,	young fellow
Cled,	clothed
Commin,	coming
Coof,	blockhead
Corlie,	to talk familiarly
Crack,	conversation
Croon,	a hollow moan
Crouse,	chearful

D

Daddie,	father

Daft,	giddy		Frae,	from
Dander,	to walk slowly		Fretit,	fretted
Deil,	devil		Frien',	friend
Ding,	to worst		Fyke,	a fuss about trifles
Doiled,	stupified			
Doon,	done		**G**	
Douse,	sober, wise,			
	prudent		Ga',	gall
Drap,	drop		Gade,	went
Drees,	feels		Gae,	go
Dreigh,	tedious		Gaet,	way, manner
Drouth,	drought		Gane,	gone
Drummock,	meal and water		Gang,	go
Dung,	pushed, driven		Gar,	to make, to force
			Gawn,	going
E			Gear,	riches, goods
			Geek,	to toss the head
Ear',	early			in scorn
E'e, een,	eye, eyes		Ghaist,	ghost
En',	end		Gie,	to give
Enow,	enough		Gied,	gave
			Gien,	given
F			Gie's,	give us
			Giglet,	a young girl
Fa',	fall		Gin,	if, against
Fan' fan'd,	found		Girts,	jerks
Fash,	to trouble,		Gloamin',	twilight
	to care for		Glour,	stare
Faun,	fallen		Goving,	gazing
Faut,	fault		Gowd,	gold
Feat,	neat, spruce		Gowk,	cuckow
Fin',	find		Gowl,	to howl
Fippence,	five pence		Graith,	accoutrements
Fisle,	bustle		Grane,	a groan
Fit,	foot		Greet,	to weep
Forfoughten,	fatigued		Grin',	grind
Forby,	beside		Grousome,	grim
Forgie,	forgive		Grumphie,	a sow
Fother,	fodder		Grun,	ground
Fou,	full		Guid,	good

Gully   a large knife
Gude,   the Supreme Being

H

Hae,   have
Haffet,   temple or side of
           the head
Hale,   whole
Hame,   home
Haud,   hold
Haun, han',   hands, hand
Hame,   home or dwelling
Haverel,   half-witted
He's,   he will
Het,   hot, made hot
Hinches,   haunches
Hin'most,   hindmost
Hizzie,   hussey
Hornie,   a name for the
           Devil
Hunner,   hundred
Hyte,   delirious

J I

I',   in
Jauk,   to trifle, dally
Ident,   diligent
Ilk' or ilka,   each, every
Ithers,   others

K

Keek,   to peep
Ken,   to know
Kintra,   country
Kittle,   to tickle
Kyte,   belly

L

Laigh,   low
Laith,   loath
Lanely,   lonely
Lang,   long
Langer,   longer
Lea'e,   leave
Lear,   learning
Leuk,   look
Lift,   sky
Lug,   ear

M

Mair,   more
Mak',   make
Mang,   to make delirious
Maun,   must
Meere,   mare
Men',   mend
Mense,   good manners
Mint,   venture
Mither,   mother
Mony,   many
Muckle,   much

N

Na,   no, not, nor
Nae,   no, not any
Naethin',   nothing
Nane,   none
Nappy,   ale
Neuk,   corner
Nieve,   fist
Niffer,   exchange
Noo,   now

O

O',   of
Ony,   any
Ought,   any thing
Ower,   over, too

P

Pit,   to put
Pickle,   small quantity
Plew,   plough
Plumpit,   plumped
Pou,   to pull
Pow,   the head, skull
Pratoes,   potatoes
Pun',   pound

Q

Quat,   to quit

R

Ramstam,   thoughtless, headlong
Raw,   row
Rig,   ridge
Rin,   to run
Row,   to roll, wrap
Rowth,   plenty
Rung,   a cudgel

S

Sae,   so
Sair,   a sore, to serve
Sakless,   innocent
Sang,   a song
Saul,   soul

Saut,   salt
Sel',   self
Selt,   sold
Shaw,   to show
Shough,   a ditch, a trench
Shool,   a shovel
Shoon,   shoes
Sic,   such - sicna, such a
Siller,   silver, money
Sin',   since
Sin,   a son
Skaith,   damage
Slee,   sly
Sleeket,   sleek, sly
Sma',   small
Snash,   abuse
Snaw,   snow
Snig,   cut
Sonsie,   lucky
Souple,   supple, swift
Souther,   solder
Spaul,   limb
Spier,   to ask, enquire
Sta',   stall
Stan' or staun,   stand
Stane,   stone
Stap,   stop
Sten,   jump
Steek,   to shut
Streak,   to stretch
Sud,   should
Syne,   since, ago, then

T

Tam,   Tom
Tak',   to take
T'ane,   the one
Tap,   top
Tauld or tald,   told

Teen,	anger
Thegither,	together
Thole,	to suffer, endure
Thoom,	thumb
Thrang,	throng
Till,	to
Timmer,	timber
Tinkler,	tinker
Tint,	spent
Tippence,	two-pence
Tither,	the other
Toom,	empty
Twa,	two
Twa three,	a few
Twal,	twelve
Twonty,	twenty

U & V

Unco,	strange
Vauntie,	boasting

W

Wab,	web of cloth
Wad,	would - a bet, to bet
Waddin',	wedding
Wadna,	would not
Wae,	woe, sorrowful
Wakerife,	wakeful
Wat,	wet - I'wat, I know
Wale,	to choose
Waur,	worse
Wee,	little
Weel,	well
Wha,	when - whon, when
Whanged,	cut off
Whare,	where
Wha'se,	whose

Whisht,	silence, to be silent
Whittle,	a knife
Wi',	with
Wie,	a little time
Win',	wind
Winna,	will not
Wingle,	wrestle
Wistna,	I know not
Withouten,	without
Wonner,	wondrous
Woodie,	a rope
Wrang,	wrong

Y

Ye,	frequently used for thou
Ye's,	you will
Yestreen,	yesternight
Yoursel,	yourself.